Free (and Almost Free) Adventures for Teenagers

Free (and Almost Free) Adventures for Teenagers

Gail L. Grand

John Wiley & Sons, Inc.
New York Chichester Brisbane Toronto Singapore

Library of Congress Cataloging-in-Publication Data
Grand, Gail L.
  Free (and almost free) adventures for teenagers/
  Gail L. Grand
    p. cm.
  Includes index.
  ISBN 0-471-11351-4 (acid-free paper)
    1. Practicums—United States—Directories. 2. Internship programs—United States—Directories. 3. Educational acceleration—United States—Directories. 4. Summer schools—United States—Directories. 5. Field work (Educational method) I. Title.
LC1072.P73G73 1995
371.3'8—dc20   95-880

Once again, for Harry, with love

Contents

Preface

Every year, tens of thousands of America's brightest young people enrich their lives, expand their intellects, and explore career opportunities through educational enrichment experiences. Programs for precollege students in subjects ranging from art to zoology are available on college campuses and at art centers and science institutes throughout the United States. Motivated students from 4th to 12th grades can find programs that will increase their knowledge of just about any subject in which they are interested. Unfortunately, many of the programs are very costly, and beyond the financial reach of most families. That's where this book can help.

Free (and Almost Free) Adventures for Teenagers is the only guide to free and very-low-cost educational enrichment programs. Most of the programs described within are provided to students at no cost; the remainder are under $200, well below the actual cost of operating the program. The majority of these programs are residential, and provide students with tuition, room, and meals on campus. Some of the programs listed even provide transportation for participants to and from campus, or may offer a small stipend to the students. Unless specified, however, the students are responsible for personal expenses and for transportation to and from the program site. All of the programs are heavily subsidized, allowing them to offer high-quality educational experiences. In addition to the academic component, these enrichment programs also provide students with an enthusiastic peer group of friends who are excited about learning, as well as counselors and instructors who serve as role models and mentors. Since summer vacation should also be fun, the programs generally offer a full range of recreational opportunities including sports, trips, and social events. All of this is available to you for $200 or less!

Summer offerings include practical, hands-on experiences such as scientific research internships, art and theater apprenticeships, field experiences, and performing arts programs in dance, music, and drama. Students can engage in intensive study of a single field or take part in critical thinking and interdisciplinary learning. Summer programs might take you to an archaeological dig site in Oregon, to an oceanographic research institute in Massachusetts, to a national park in Alaska, to a college campus in Virginia, or to an aerospace laboratory at NASA. You might find yourself part of a community of artists in South Carolina, on a cultural exchange program in Russia, or a member of a scientific research team in California. The subject and location indexes will help you to find the programs that are perfect for you.

The school year presents additional opportunities. Internships, research programs, distance-learning opportunities, school-break adventures, enrichment classes, workshops, and acceleration programs all offer motivated young people the chance to enrich their education. Many of the school year programs supplement your regular academic schedule, while others provide intensive enrichment experiences during school vacation periods and weekends. In Part Two you'll find programs representative of the opportunities that await interested students during the regular academic year.

Browse through the book, spending more time on those programs that interest you. Read the personal accounts of students, like yourselves, who have participated in some of the experiences described here. Their words will help you to understand the tremendous impact enrichment programs can have on your life. Several indexes have been included to ease your search for the programs best suited to you. These indexes will lead you to programs by subject, location, and program type. There is a separate index to programs for special populations such as women, minority students, and the gifted and talented.

Contact the coordinator of the programs that interest you and consider their offerings carefully. All material presented here has been drawn from the programs' informational publications and is as up-to-date as possible. However, course offerings sometimes change, or there may be revisions in program or application dates, length, or fees. Most of the offerings are sponsored or hosted by universities and art and science institutes. These programs provide students with the opportunity to try out life as a college student. Some are funded by governmental agencies and private industry and generally offer participants a firsthand view of career opportunities in that industry. Students and their parents are advised to investigate and evaluate the suitability of the individual programs they choose; the author does not endorse or evaluate any of the programs described in this book.

Parents, teachers, and counselors serve on the front lines as providers of information, as mentors, and as advisers. I encourage all of you to use this book as a resource to guide students to experiences that may provide a career direction, kindle a lifelong interest, or perhaps change a teen's life.

Through the writing and publication of this resource guide, I have sought to reach out to you, our nation's most capable students, and make you aware of the opportunities that are available. These "bargains in education" can enrich your lives beyond measure. Like Richard Johnston, a former student at the South Carolina Governor's School for the Arts, you may discover "the most valuable artistic and cultural experience of [your] life". Richard discovered through his experience "that art, in all its diverse forms and styles, is a glorification of life and the human spirit." Whatever your own area of interest—the arts, the sciences, the humanities—I hope you'll use this book as the first step in your own voyage of discovery. Happy hunting!

Acknowledgments

I am very grateful to all of the individuals who helped in the preparation of this book. My editor at John Wiley & Sons, Kate Bradford, deserves the first thanks, since she suggested the subject, and then watched over the book on the long road from inception to publication. Thank you, Kate, for both the idea and its execution.

The programs described in this book have been developed and are led by some of the most enthusiastic educators in the country. They've sent me informational material and program brochures, and have suggested sources of additional information. I couldn't possibly mention all who've helped, but I'd be remiss if I didn't especially thank Dr. Virginia Simmons, West Virginia Governor's Schools; Dr. Joseph Marshall, Marine Science Consortium; Dr. Virginia Uldrick, South Carolina Governor's School; Dr. Jeff Gottfried, Oregon Museum of Science and Industry; and Jean Olson, Vermont Governor's Schools, for their valuable input and enthusiasm. Richard Johnston's thoughtful letter provided insight into the ways in which students benefit from enrichment programs.

The students profiled in this book willingly took on the task of describing their program from the participant's point of view. Their candid assessments speak to their peers in ways that I cannot. It's an accurate measure of their enthusiastic response to these programs when I tell you that they all wrote their essays and submitted them before the deadline date. Many thanks are due to Joy Basewiez, Raina Croff, Joshua Deutsch, Jeff Morneau, Joel Rosner, and Tosha Wheeler: With your words, you'll influence the lives of others.

Finally, my thanks go to my family. Alissa and Tracy who served as all-around cheerleaders and moral supporters, offering long-distance advice and encouragement. Paul, as always, acted as technical adviser and personal computer consultant, then patiently taught and guided me as I made just about every computer mistake possible. Someday, Paul, I promise I'll actually read those program manuals. And finally, thank you, Harry, for listening to my gripes, for understanding my inattentiveness, for editing text and offering ideas, and for being there for me. Thank you all.

Part One: Summer Adventures

Something very exciting is happening in American education! Each summer, tens of thousands of our most gifted young people can be found working not on deepening their tans, but instead on expanding their minds. Rather than channel surfing or hanging out at the local mall, these highly motivated teenagers spend their school breaks on college campuses, in research laboratories. Some students intern in possible future career areas while others are engaged in field studies in programs located throughout the world.

In Maryland, middle school students are thrust into the high-powered world of international negotiations, and can be found discussing such critical issues as human rights, world health, and weapons proliferation.

Outstanding high school math students from across the United States come together at a summer program hosted by a Texas university to take the advanced mathematics courses unavailable to them at their home schools. Along the way, they discover that lots of other young people think math is "cool."

Extraordinary young dancers spend their summer days in studio classes, seminars, and workshops, studying with professional artists and master teachers at arts programs in California, Illinois, Kentucky, Minnesota, New Jersey, Pennsylvania, South Carolina, and Vermont. In the evenings they attend lectures, concerts, and readings, and view performances by guest artists. Together with other talented young people, they share in the creative excitement generated by living in a community of artists.

Hearing-impaired high school students find future careers in an exciting four week program in which they study marine biology, oceanology, animal behavior, and coastal ecology. Both their minds and self-esteem grow through hands-on experiences in the waters, the field, and the laboratories of the Marine Science Consortium facility at Wallops Island, Virginia.

All of these young people have chosen to take an active role in their own education. Each supplements his or her school year learning through participation in an educational enrichment program. You, too, can be an active learner; consider this book to be your passport to adventure!

Benefits

Perhaps you're still not quite sure that you want to give up any of your precious vacation to take part in a summer study program. Let's take a look at some of the benefits you can expect from participation in an educational enrichment program.

Summer programs can offer you experiences impossible to duplicate during the school year. You might find yourself doing archaeological fieldwork in Colorado or attending scientific talks at the space science center in Kaliningrad,

Russia. Perhaps you'd enjoy working with professional planners and community leaders to plan future uses for a 5200-acre development site in Michigan, or you'd like to learn firsthand about cultural differences and community service through participation in an international workcamp in India. Whatever subject or discipline you'd like to explore, there is a summer program that will engage your time and whet your interest for further study.

Summer programs allow you to take an early, realistic look at future career opportunities. Instead of just dreaming of a future as a writer or dancer, as a doctor or lawyer, you can actually explore these careers and determine if they fit well with your abilities, interests, and personality characteristics. Through field trips to work sites, research laboratories, museums, theater companies, and local industries, you can get a close-up view of the real world applications of your studies. Many of the summer programs also provide career counseling. Visiting professionals offer insights into their careers and act as mentors and role models.

Summer programs held on college campuses also provide participants with opportunities to develop a close student-mentor relationship with university faculty members and graduate students. These individuals can serve as advisors to guide you on your career path and may eventually become part of your professional network. Because they are knowledgeable about what it takes to become a member of a specific profession, they are in an ideal position to direct you to appropriate colleges and opportunities for continuing education.

Taking part in a summer program affords you the luxury of total immersion into a single area of study. During the school year, your day is fragmented into six or more different subject areas; little time can be devoted to any one field. In an intensive summer experience, you can choose to attend a program that will allow you to spend most of your time studying dance or computers, microbiology or TV production, mathematics or international relations. You'll have access to the most up-to-date equipment and the latest technological advances in your field of interest. Perhaps best of all, you'll be surrounded by other young people who have similar interests, and for whom it is OK to be smart.

Still another benefit of summer participation is the potential to get a taste of college life before you actually become a college student. You'll try out life in a dormitory, learn the perils of time and money management, and discover firsthand what it means to be responsible for seeing to your own needs such as laundry and meals. Many of the programs award college credit for your summer studies, so participation in several programs may allow you to enter college as much as a full semester ahead. Program participants are also encouraged to use the host institution's recreational, computer, library, studio, and laboratory facilities, and most of the programs have a full social and recreational component. In addition, you'll have the benefits of readily accessible peers; friends are always available when you want to play tennis, go for a swim, or shoot some baskets.

Finally, participation in a summer enrichment program may give you an edge in the college admissions process and in the quest for scholarships. If you dream of attending a very selective institution, devoting your vacation time to study demonstrates your serious commitment to education. Your experiences during the summer may become the focus of a required application essay or perhaps will evolve into a science fair project, a published piece of creative writing, or be incorporated into a research paper. You may also choose to have one of your summer college professors write a letter of recommendation for you to the college of your choice. The words of someone familiar with your ability to do college-level work carry a good deal of weight. Sometimes, participation in these summer programs affords students the opportunity to become eligible for college scholarships. Certainly, the summer will be like no other learning experience that you have ever had. Participation in an educational enrichment program can affect the way you view education, challenge your ideas about your future, and perhaps even change the direction of your life.

About Money

The enrichment programs described in this book have been specifically chosen to be affordable. Although intellectually stimulating summer programs are offered at numerous colleges and universities across the United States, many of these opportunities may be financially beyond the reach of all but the most affluent students. Some programs offer financial aid, but this aid is generally reserved for minority and disadvantaged students, and is not generally available to students from middle-income backgrounds.

Quality educational programs are very expensive to establish and operate. The actual cost of providing students with housing, meals, instruction, supervision, materials, and extracurricular trips and activities during a summer program averages between $500 and $600 per student per week. All of the summer opportunities described in this book are available to students at little or no cost. Some also provide students with transportation expenses, and participants may even receive a small stipend to replace money that might have been earned through a summer job.

Using the Listings

The summer programs included in this Part have been divided into three chapters. Programs in the first chapter, the humanities, include selections that focus on the visual arts (drawing, painting, sculpture), the performing arts (music, dance, theater), journalism, creative writing, communications, foreign languages, the social sciences (psychology, sociology), business, and architecture.

The second chapter in Part I features the sciences, mathematics, and technology. Here you'll find programs that specialize in engineering, computer science, mathematics, robotics, the physical sciences (chemistry and physics), the earth sciences (geology, meteorology, astronomy), the life sciences (biology, genetics, agriculture, marine science), and environmental science.

The last chapter of Part I, comprehensive programs, includes programs that feature both the arts and sciences, as well as foreign exchange programs, volunteer opportunities, and interdisciplinary studies.

Each listing provides detailed information about the specific program, as well as a paragraph describing the activities that are part of the experience. The listings are organized alphabetically in each section by program title. If you are looking for a particular field of study, such as sculpture, business, Japanese language, or health science, check the Index by Subject at the end of the book for programs offering that field of study. The Index to Programs for Special Populations will direct you to opportunities especially designed for gifted and talented students, for women, or for minority students. If you are limited to attending programs in a specific geographical region, you will find the State Index to be helpful.

Information supplied in the listings includes:

Host School: Most of these programs are held on college campuses or at scientific research laboratories and field sites.

Type: Describes the program's focus. Offerings may be described as academic enrichment, internship, field experience, volunteer opportunity, art classes, creative writing workshop, etc.

Location: Indicates where the program is held.

Duration: Indicates length of program. Longer programs are more likely to offer college credit.

Dates: Only approximate dates are listed since specific dates may vary from year to year. Contact the programs in which you are interested for this summer's dates.

Qualifications: The grade levels listed refer to the grade student will be entering during the fall following the program. Occasionally, qualified applicants one grade level below those listed may be accepted. Ages refer to student's age at time of program unless otherwise specified.

Although all programs seek students who are especially interested in the program's focus, some offerings have specific requirements. Some are limited to students from a specific geographic region while others are reserved for minority or women students. Some programs require academic qualifications, for example, identification as academically gifted, or creatively talented.

Housing: Although programs often include provision for commuter participants, most of the opportunities described in this book provide residential housing. On college campuses, this generally means living in a dormitory reserved for students of high school or middle school age. These dormitories are supervised by resident advisors or counselors associated either with the host college or the program; more supervision is provided for younger students. Meals are provided in most cases, and supervised evening and weekend activities are an integral part of the program.

Living accommodations on field programs, volunteer opportunities, and traveling programs are often Spartan. You might find yourself living in a group dormitory or in a tent. However, some of the most rustic housing is found in the most spectacular natural settings.

Costs: All of the programs listed in this book are provided to students at relatively little or no cost. The cost listed includes fees for tuition, instructional materials, room, meals, and activities, unless otherwise noted in the listing. The majority of the programs are totally free; students will only need small amounts of personal spending money for incidental expenses. Parents are generally expected to supply transportation to and from the program site. In some cases, students will receive a stipend for their participation and/or money for transportation expenses. Almost all of the programs have provisions for awarding need-based financial aid.

Credits given: Indicates if college or high school credits are available. Students will need to secure the approval of their home schools to obtain high school credit for participation.

Contact: Write to (or phone) the contact listed for the programs in which you are interested and request a program brochure and application. After reading the complete brochures, you will be able to determine which programs best suit you.

A descriptive paragraph concludes each listing, describing the program, listing areas of study and activity options, and providing a look at how the program is structured. Application deadlines are included when available. If no date appears, a call to the program coordinator will provide a closing date. Please note, however, that it is always better to complete your application as early as possible; many of the programs accept applicants on a rolling basis, filling places as qualified applicants apply. The later your application, the poorer your chance of acceptance. Occasionally, a program is not filled by the date listed; a phone call after that date will allow you to determine if space is still available.

Scattered throughout the book, you'll find profiles of students who have actually taken part in some of these programs. Their words will provide a student's eye view of what the summer experience meant to them.

Local Opportunities

If you cannot or do not wish to leave home this summer, how can you find out about local programs? If you are interested in a study program, call colleges, universities, or community colleges in your area and inquire about the availability of such programs. You might try contacting either the special program office or the office of continuing education. Even if no organized program exists, you may be able to take college-level courses as a special student. Also, check with your school guidance counselor. Your counselor may know of local opportunities, such as governor's programs or internships, that welcome commuter students. You might also call or write to your State Department of Education for additional options.

Another possibility is to check with local institutions such as science or art museums, local theatre companies, science institutes, the Department of Parks and Recreation, the National Park Service, or local chapters of environmental groups such as Greenpeace, or political action committees that may meet in your area. These organizations often offer local students the opportunity to participate in summer courses or internships. If your interest is in scientific research, you may be able to arrange your own laboratory experience. Try contacting the volunteer office or science research facilities at your area hospital and offer your services as an unpaid science intern. If you're interested in the health sciences, call your local veterinarian, optometrist, podiatrist, dentist, or medical doctor and ask if you can work as an apprentice. Students interested in careers in the media might check on internship opportunities at community newspapers, local TV stations, magazines, or film production companies. Budding artists might opt for positions as apprentices to local artists. Spending your summer interning on a job may not provide you with funds, but the knowledge you gain about career opportunities and the relationship you develop with a mentor may be far more rewarding than dollars. You will also gain insight into the real world applications of your area of interest and begin to build a resume. Here's to a great, intellectually stimulating, and rewarding summer experience!

Humanities

Arkansas International Languages Program

Students who are chosen for this program spend two weeks totally immersed in the language and culture of the countries in which their chosen language is spoken. On arrival, students are issued a simulated "passport" permitting entry into their country. All sessions are held in university facilities decorated to reflect a foreign atmosphere. Language instruction focuses on vocabulary and speaking structures needed to participate in community life, with practice periods interspersed with activities that include singing, dancing, sports, cooking, and crafts. Personal spending is conducted using foreign currency, and all meals served are typical of those eaten by people living in Spanish- and German-speaking countries. Interested students need to apply through their local school guidance counselor. ***Contact the program coordinator for application deadlines.***

Host School:	Arkansas Tech University
Type:	French, Spanish, and German Language Programs
Location:	Russellville, AR
Duration:	Two weeks
Dates:	French: Mid-June. Spanish: Late June through early July. German: Mid- to late July.
Qualifications:	Entering grades 9 through 11. Open to Arkansas students on a competitive application basis.
Housing:	Participants are housed in air-conditioned dormitories and are provided with all meals.
Costs:	None
Credits Given:	None
Contact:	Dan McElderry
	Arkansas International Languages Program
	Arkansas Tech University
	116-D Dean Hall
	Russellville, AR 72801-2222
	(501) 968-0807; FAX (501) 964-0812

Arts and Sciences at Adrian College Arts Focus: Performing, Communication, and Visual Arts

Students explore the program's theme of the interrelationship between humanity and the environment from an arts perspective. Participants choose a focus area from fields of study that include improvisational theater, creative writing, environmental journalism, dance, environmental sculpture, and landscape architecture. Activities performed in each of these areas include the creation and production of a theater piece that informs others about the environment; the exploration of oneself through the writing, sharing, and critiquing of poetry, short stories, and drama; the communication of current and complex material through informative journalism; creative movement for expression; the creation of small and large sculptures using media that includes clay, adobe, and handmade paper; and the use of landscape techniques and design to protect our fragile ecosystem. Discussion groups, hands-on activities, field experiences, research trips, simulations, and speakers all combine to provide participants with a new perspective on environmental concerns. Recreational activities are part of the program. Apply through your guidance counselor. ***Application deadline: March 1.***

Host School:	Adrian College
Type:	Fine and Performing Arts
Location:	Adrian, MI
Duration:	Two weeks
Dates:	End of June through mid-July
Qualifications:	Entering grades 11 and 12. Open to Michigan public and private school students.
Housing:	Participants are housed in the residence halls and have meals in the dining hall.
Costs:	$200. Need-based financial aid is also available.
Credits Given:	None
Contact:	Arts and Sciences at Adrian College
	Adrian College
	110 South Madison
	Adrian, MI 49221
	(517) 265-5161

CAPA: Creative and Performing Arts

Talented Arkansas middle school students can participate in an intensive two-week study of the arts through the CAPA program. Students focus on one major area of study, choosing from selections that include the visual arts, theater and drama, creative writing, and pottery, but also engage in exploration activities in all areas. Activities include enrichment sessions, supervised readings, debates, reviews on the history of art, and examining man's need to create. Presentations by guest speakers, along with field trips to museums, art galleries, plays, and to the studios of local artists, provide students with a close look at art today. Upon the completion of CAPA, students exhibit their own works of art and participate in an original theatrical production, produced and directed by CAPA students. CAPA is part of Arkansas' AEGIS program (Academic Enrichment for the Gifted in Summer). ***Contact the program coordinator for application information.***

Host School:	DeQueen-Mena ESC
Type:	Creative and Performing Arts
Location:	Mena, AR
Duration:	Two weeks
Dates:	Late July through early August
Qualifications:	Entering grades 7 through 9. Open to Arkansas students talented in the arts.
Housing:	Participants are housed in a local facility and are provided with meals.
Costs:	None
Credits Given:	None
Contact:	Martha Cathey
	CAPA: Creative and Performing Arts
	DeQueen-Mena ESC
	P.O. Box 110
	Hornbeck Road
	Gillham, AR 71841
	(501) 386-2251; FAX (501) 386-7731

Columbia College High School Summer Institute

Students serious about the arts can choose to take classes taught by working professionals at Columbia College Chicago. Each course offers hands-on practical experience in the student's area of interest. Fine arts students might choose from selections that include graphic design, fashion design, interior design, computer graphics, and mixed media. Communications students might opt for courses in poetry writing, fiction writing, news reporting, film techniques, or an animation workshop. Management classes are offered in record production, the fashion industry, and advertising. Courses in music, photography, dance workshop, and acting and improvisational techniques, are also available. Students interested in the electronic media may choose to take television, radio, or audio production classes. All of these offerings go far beyond programs available to high school students at their home schools, thus providing participants with a focused look at careers in the arts. After-class activities may find students exploring Chicago, as they take part in free excursions to concerts, walking tours, and trips to the Omnimax and Oceanarium. A showcase of all students' work and pizza party culminate the summer program. ***Rolling admissions.***

Host School: Columbia College Chicago
Type: Fine, Performing, and Communications Arts
Location: Chicago, IL
Duration: Six weeks
Dates: Early July through mid-August
Qualifications: Entering grades 10 through 12, and entering college freshmen. Open to any student with a serious interest in the fine arts, performing arts, media arts, or communication arts.
Housing: This is a nonresidential program. Out-of-town participants may contact the program for help in locating housing.
Costs: $200 for 2 credit courses, $360 for 3 credit courses. (Most courses carry 2 credits.) A limited number of scholarships are available.
Credits Given: 2–3 college credits
Contact: Columbia College High School Summer Institute
Columbia College Chicago
600 South Michigan Avenue
Chicago, IL 60605-1996
(312) 663-1600, ext 134

Counselor Program

Ramapo Anchorage Camp is a not-for-profit charitable residential summer camp serving emotionally disturbed and learning-impaired children. Children ages four to fourteen are referred by social service agencies, mental health professionals, and special educators. Ramapo provides a therapeutic, highly structured environment, fostering the development of positive social and learning skills. An overall one-to-one counselor-to-camper ratio helps children experience success. The children participate in creative projects, sports, and outdoor experiences. They are encouraged to have fun, acquire new skills, and to behave within normal limits. The camp provides a comprehensive orientation program for counselors, and offers ongoing training in working with and understanding the needs of handicapped children. In addition to the program, the State University of New York at New Paltz offers two fieldwork and seminar courses to counselors free of charge: the child psychology course entitled "Field Experience with Emotionally Disturbed Children" and the teaching skills class "Educating Children with Emotional and Learning Disabilities." Each carries 3 credits. Counselors find working at Ramapo to be intense and demanding, but also unusually enriching and rewarding. ***Contact program for application information.***

Host School:	Ramapo Anchorage Camp
Type:	Camp Counselor for Emotionally Disturbed and Learning-Impaired Children
Location:	Rhinebeck, NY
Duration:	Two months
Dates:	Late June through late August
Qualifications:	Entering grade 12. (Most of the counseling staff is composed of college students.) The program is suited for caring, energetic young men and women who are interested in careers in the human services. Students work with children who are experiencing a wide range of emotional, behavioral, and learning problems.
Housing:	Counselors are housed in cabins with other campers. Meals are taken in the dining hall.
Costs:	None. Counselors receive a small salary based on education, skill, and experience.
Credits Given:	6 college credits may be earned free of charge for courses taken while at camp. Arrangements may also be made for independent studies credits.
Contact:	Counselor Program Ramapo Anchorage Camp P.O. Box 266 Rhinebeck, NY 12572 (914) 876-8403

Criminal Justice, Law Enforcement, and Investigative Technology: Michigan Summer Institute

This summer institute exposes students to the entire spectrum of criminal justice fields, including investigative technologies, crime, prosecution, the courts, and correction facilities. Participants in this unique program explore the criminal justice system through team problem-solving activities. Activities include crime scene investigation, hostage negotiation, SWAT team exercises, and climbing and rappelling. Students get a close look at the criminal justice system as it operates in the real world with visits to the State Crime Laboratory, the Juvenile Probate Court, and area correction facilities. Students will also spend time in firearm safety and target practice at the ballistics range and can sail through Delta's Sailing School. Social, cultural, and recreational programs are provided. For further information, contact Craig Beins at (517) 686-9109 or see information below. *Application deadline: February 28.*

Host School:	Delta College
Type:	Criminal Justice
Location:	University Center, MI
Duration:	One week
Dates:	Beginning of August
Qualifications:	Entering grades 11 and 12. Open to Michigan students interested in the criminal justice system.
Housing:	Participants are housed in dormitories and have meals in the dining facilities.
Costs:	$200. Financial aid is available.
Credits Given:	None
Contact:	Chris Kitzman
	Criminal Justice, Law Enforcement, and Investigative Technology
	Ingham Intermediate School District
	2630 West Howell Road
	Mason, MI 48854
	(517) 676-2550

East Carolina Summer Theater Apprentice Program

Here's a challenge for the student serious about theater—an opportunity to work long hours for no pay, coupled with the chance to see if the participant is suited for the demands and rewards of professional theater. Student apprentices receive a week of training in shop and stage practices, and then spend the summer working in the various shops, helping with scenery construction and painting props, working with lights and costumes. Apprentices have no opportunity to perform; this is not an acting program. However, they may serve as assistants to stage managers in rehearsals, and they do serve as running crews for all shows. The average workday runs from 9 A.M. to at least 10:30 P.M., so students need to be prepared for an intensive summer experience. Benefits include the opportunity to observe working professionals practicing their craft at one of the premier programs in the region, as well as earn a professional resume credit. *Application deadline: April 8.*

Host School:	East Carolina University
Type:	Theater Production Apprentice Program
Location:	Greenville, NC
Duration:	Up to seven and one-half weeks
Dates:	Early June through late July
Qualifications:	At least 16 years of age. Open to students interested in gaining practical working experience in theater production.
Housing:	Participants are housed in a university dormitory.
Costs:	None. Apprentices are responsible for their own meals.
Credits Given:	Credits are available through East Carolina University at additional cost.
Contact:	Jay Herzog
	East Carolina Summer Theater Apprentice Program
	East Carolina University
	Department of Theater Arts
	Greenville, NC 27858
	(919) 757-6390

Fulbright School of Public Affairs

The Fulbright School provides students interested in public affairs with the opportunity to examine current social, economic, and political conditions, and to consider the meaning of civic responsibility in a democratic society. Students study the influence of cultural values and traditions on politics and public policy and consider the role of the media in shaping public opinion. Through meetings with politicians, state officials, lobbyists, and university faculty, the students learn how they can become more involved in policy making. Program activities include simulations, projects, exercises, and sessions that focus on the development of more effective communication skills. ***Contact the program coordinator for application information.***

Host School:	University of Arkansas
Type:	Public Affairs
Location:	Fayetteville, AR
Duration:	Three weeks
Dates:	Early July through end of July
Qualifications:	Entering grade 12. Open to gifted and talented Arkansas students interested in politics and public affairs.
Housing:	Participants are housed in the dormitories and have meals in the dining hall.
Costs:	None
Credits Given:	None
Contact:	Betty Guhman
	Fulbright School of Public Affairs
	University of Arkansas
	Sociology Department
	211 Main Street
	Fayetteville, AR 72701
	(501) 575-3205

G/C/TV: Green County Television

Participants in the G/C/TV program have an opportunity to develop their verbal, nonverbal, and written communication skills in this exciting program, presented through the AEGIS (Academic Enrichment for the Gifted in Summer) program. G/C/TV students are involved in producing a newscast in which all jobs, including writers, camera operators, director, and newscasters, are filled by students. Participants get hands-on, practical experience in broadcast TV, as they research the timely issues affecting national, international, and local news. In addition, students will develop a variety of segments for the newscast, from sports and medicine to commercials. ***Contact program coordinator for application deadline.***

Host School:	Green County Technical Schools
Type:	Communications and Broadcast TV
Location:	Paragould, AR
Duration:	Three weeks
Dates:	Mid-June through early July
Qualifications:	Entering grades 9 through 11. Open to Arkansas students interested in the world of electronic broadcasting.
Housing:	Participants are housed in the Green County area and are provided with meals.
Costs:	None
Credits Given:	None
Contact:	Kem Drake
	G/C/TV
	Green County Technical Schools
	5201 West King's Highway
	Paragould, AR 72450
	(501) 236-6113

High School Journalism Workshop

High school journalists holding key editorial positions such as editor-in-chief, managing editor, and features editor may take part in this hands-on workshop offered by the E. W. Scripps School of Journalism. Seminars address topics that include investigative reporting, broadcast journalism, circulation management, advertising sales, and desktop publishing. Student assignments provide experience in newspaper writing, design, and news judgment. Participants are taught by both award-winning high school newspaper advisers and Ohio University journalism professors. Participants have the use of the School of Journalism's computer writing and graphics laboratory. ***Rolling admissions. Apply early.***

Host School:	Ohio University
Type:	Journalism Workshop
Location:	Athens, OH
Duration:	Three days
Dates:	Mid-June
Qualifications:	High school journalism students. Applicants must hold key editorial positions for the coming school year.
Housing:	Participants are housed in the residence halls and have meals in the dining halls. Curfew is 11:00 P.M.
Costs:	$99
Credits Given:	One quarter hour of college-level journalism credit for seniors.
Contact:	High School Journalism Workshop
	Ohio University
	Memorial Auditorium
	Athens, OH 45701-2979
	(614) 593-2591; FAX (614) 593-2592

Indian People of Arkansas and Their Neighbors

In this unusual program, students camp and work for one week at Ouachita National Forest, at a bluff shelter site, as members of the Arkansas Archaeological Society. While at the field site, students visit prehistoric and historic areas, participate in excavations, and practice Native American crafts such as flint-knapping, spear-throwing, and basketry. During the second week of the program, the students study on campus at Southern Arkansas University, utilizing their experiences as a means of improving their writing and communication skills. This program is presented as part of Arkansas' AEGIS (Academic Enrichment for the Gifted in Summer) program. ***Contact program coordinator for application information and deadline.***

Host School:	Southern Arkansas University
Type:	Archaeology and Native American Studies
Location:	Magnolia, AR
Duration:	Two weeks
Dates:	Middle through late July
Qualifications:	Entering grades 11 and 12. Open to Arkansas students.
Housing:	Participants camp out at Ouachita National Forest during the first part of the program. Housing in the campus dormitories is provided during the second week. Meals are provided.
Costs:	None
Credits Given:	None
Contact:	Mary Hamilton
	Indian People of Arkansas and Their Neighbors
	Southern Arkansas University
	Box 1389
	Magnolia, AR 71753
	(501) 235-4186

KEMPA Summer Journalism Workshop

Each summer, students from across Wisconsin and Illinois travel to the University of Wisconsin, Whitewater, to attend the Kettle Moraine Press Association's Summer Journalism Workshop. Large group sessions involving all the journalism students provide exposure to other aspects of scholastic journalism. Small group sessions in core areas provide students with the specialized information they need to become better journalists. Students choose courses in one of the three forms of journalism offered: newspaper, yearbook, and photojournalism. Classes are grouped according to prior experience. The newspaper workshop offers classes in basic newswriting, beginning and experienced feature writing, opinion writing, sports, in-depth reporting and staff management, and newspaper layout and design. Yearbook students may focus on beginning design and writing, copy-writing, theme development and staff management, and layout and design. Photojournalists receive instruction in the fundamentals of photography, darkroom procedures, exposure, criteria of good photography, and principles and ethics. Recreational time is provided in the program's busy schedule. *Registration deadline: May 20. (Workshops cost $10 more after this date, if space is available.)*

Host School:	University of Wisconsin, Whitewater
Type:	Journalism Workshops
Location:	Whitewater, WI
Duration:	One week
Dates:	Mid-July
Qualifications:	High school students. Open to both beginning and experienced high school journalists, with classes grouped by experience.
Housing:	Participants are housed in a residence hall and have meals in the dining facilities.
Costs:	$200 for yearbook or newspaper workshops; $220 for photojournalism workshop; $230 for desktop publishing. This fee includes instruction, room, and three meals a day. Students who prefer a package without meals may deduct $30 from the workshop price.
Credits Given:	None
Contact:	KEMPA Summer Journalism Workshop
	University of Wisconsin, Whitewater
	Continuing Education Services
	2005 Roseman
	Whitewater, WI 53190
	(414) 472-3165; FAX (414) 472-5210

Kentucky Governor's School of the Arts (GSA)

Students serious about and gifted in the arts have an opportunity to spend three weeks in an intensive arts program, living and learning from master teachers in a supportive community of artists. Students engage in an intensive study in one of six artistic disciplines: creative writing, dance, drama, instrumental music, visual art, or vocal music. Students attend daily seminars in their field of specialization and participate in master classes, lectures, workshops, and field trips. Interdisciplinary art experiences familiarize all students with the joys and challenges of the other artistic areas.

The faculty, made up of professional teaching artists, are chosen for their ability to act as both teachers and mentors for the young artists attending the program. Outstanding guest artists serve as visiting faculty, presenting master classes, lectures, and performances at the school. College and career counseling, both during and following the program, provide opportunities for further study. A Student Performance Festival and Graduation is held at the Kentucky Center for the Arts at the end of the summer program. Admission auditions are held at selected sites across the state during January. *Contact the program director for application information and deadlines.*

Host School:	Bellarmine College
Type:	Fine and Performing Arts
Location:	Louisville, KY
Duration:	Three weeks
Dates:	Late June through mid-July
Qualifications:	Entering grades 11 and 12. Open to Kentucky students talented in the arts. The program is competitive; only one-tenth of all applicants are selected.
Housing:	Participants are housed in dormitories and have meals in the dining hall.
Costs:	None
Credits Given:	None
Contact:	Susan Carter Knight
	Kentucky Governor's School of the Arts
	Bellarmine College
	Kentucky Center for the Arts
	5 Riverfront Plaza
	Louisville, KY 40202-2989
	(502) 562-0729

KINSHIP: A Summer Connection to Nonwestern Architecture

In a unique program directed to minority students, Florida A & M University offers participants a chance to explore diversity in architectural style, while getting an introduction to architecture and architectural careers. The program focuses on Asian, North and West African, Latin, and Middle Eastern architecture. In addition to learning the basics of architecture, students get a close look at real-world career opportunities through visits to professional offices, construction sites, museums and historic sites, and video presentations. Guest lecturers serve as role models. The program also includes weekend trips. **Contact program coordinator for application deadline.**

Host School:	Florida A & M University
Type:	Architecture
Location:	Tallahassee, FL
Duration:	Two weeks
Dates:	Middle through end of July
Qualifications:	Entering grades 11 and 12. Open to Florida minority students interested in exploring career opportunities in the field of architecture.
Housing:	Participants are housed in dormitories and have meals in the dining hall.
Costs:	None. Optional on-campus housing, dining services, and use of recreational facilities are provided by the university for a small fee.
Credits Given:	None
Contact:	Andrew Chin
	KINSHIP
	Florida A & M University
	Tallahassee, FL 32307
	(904) 599-3244

Minnesota Arts eXperience (MAX Summer Academy)

Here's a program designed for creative high school students who want to express themselves in their own way. Students pick one of three artistic areas in which to specialize: theater, imaginative writing, and the visual arts. Theater students study acting, voice, movement, and characterization, while exploring basic theater theory and technique. There are lots of opportunities for performance, including both ensemble and small-group work. The writer's workshop encourages participants to sharpen their skills through journals, autobiography, and creative nonfiction. Students explore reading, writing, and thinking, based on their individual experiences. Visual arts students explore their creative side through finger drawing, painting, printmaking, 3-D design, exhibition, and performance art. Out-of-class time is spent on field trips, cultural activities, and group sessions. *Application deadline: May 10.*

Host School:	Moorhead State University (MSU)
Type:	Arts Workshops
Location:	Moorhead, MN
Duration:	Two weeks
Dates:	Mid-June through beginning of July
Qualifications:	Entering grades 9 through 12. Open to all, but preference is given to Minnesota residents.
Housing:	Participants are housed in the residence halls and have meals at the campus food service.
Costs:	Registration fees based on income: $50, family income less than $30,000; $100, family income $30,000–$50,000; $150, family income above $50,000. Students outside of Minnesota pay $150. Housing: $104. Meals are the responsibility of the student. Limited financial aid is available.
Credits Given:	None
Contact:	Minnesota Arts eXperience (MAX Summer Academy) Moorhead State University Moorhead, MN 56563 (218) 236-2764; FAX (218) 299-5887

Minnesota Arts eXperience (MAX) Summer Programs

Each summer, the Minnesota Arts eXperience (MAX) programs provide more than 1700 students the opportunity to explore dance, literary arts, music, theater, media arts, and visual arts, at sites across the state. These programs offer a broad range of learning, from direct creative experience in the arts, to intensive study and personal reflection. In past summers, theater offerings have included acting and playmaking workshops, introductory acting classes, improvisational classes, community theater involvement, and summer theater. The visual arts are presented by professional artists with studio workshops that include drawing and watercolor classes, clay and pottery workshops, computer-generated art workshops, and a hand papermaking workshop. Dance offerings have included dance theater as well as workshops in ballet, jazz, tap, Afro-Caribbean dance, and modern dance. Music classes have included computer-based music composition, piano camp, oboe classes, band camp, string and chamber music, and jazz and folk music workshops. Students interested in the literary arts could choose from a young playwrights workshop, bookwriting courses, and creative writing classes. Media arts experiences have included animation workshops, visual journals, and a course in video arts. In addition to specialized offerings, a variety of interdisciplinary art experiences are also available. ***Contact program coordinator for a complete listing of upcoming offerings.***

Host School: Minnesota Center for Arts Education

Type: Summer Arts Programs

Location: Various sites throughout Minnesota

Duration: One to ten weeks

Dates: Programs are offered throughout the summer months.

Qualifications: Entering grades K through 12. Open to all Minnesota students, as well as artists and educators interested in learning together.

Housing: Housing and meals are provided on site for some of the programs. Many are offered to local commuter students only.

Costs: MAX programs are inexpensive (most cost between $10 and $150), or offered free of charge to participants.

Credits Given: Some programs offer high school credit.

Contact: Minnesota Arts eXperience (MAX) Summer Programs
Minnesota Center for Arts Education
6125 Olson Memorial Highway
Golden Valley, MN 55422
(800) 657-3515 or (612) 591-4711; FAX (612) 591-4747

Minnesota Governor's Scholars Program

The Minnesota Governor's Scholars Summer Institute is designed to develop the citizens and leaders of the next generation by providing a year of learning experiences focusing on "creating communities which value all people." Students take part in experiential learning opportunities that focus on a variety of multicultural perspectives and views on selected issues. Participants consider topics that include the American Indian perspective on the environment, the Asian perspective on families and world peace, and the African-American perspective on violence and crime. Students learn to integrate these geographic and cultural perspectives as they focus on leadership and prepare service projects to eliminate racism. Sessions include problem awareness, planning and budgeting, public speaking, ethics, value clarification, and cultural relations. These sessions help the students as they examine the impact of racism on health, business, education, the arts, technology, and social welfare. Recreational activities, dances, videos, and sports activities are planned by the students. Through this program, students learn leadership, continuous quality improvement, community organization and problem solving skills, and culturally sensitive approaches to public issues. During their senior year, each student develops and delivers a service program to advance the theme that they implement at their home school or within their community. The Governor's Scholars meet during a winter reunion in February to report on their project and share their experiences with one another. *Application deadline: April 1.*

Host School:	The Summer Institute is held on a Minnesota college campus
Type:	Leadership and Service Institute
Location:	Various sites across Minnesota
Duration:	One week summer institute plus a weekend winter institute
Dates:	Summer Institute: Early August. Winter Institute: Early February.
Qualifications:	Students currently in grade 11. Open to Minnesota students interested in community service who have the potential for leadership and a minimum 3.0 grade point average. Students are nominated by their schools to become Governor's Scholars.
Housing:	Participants are housed in residence halls and have meals in the dining facilities.
Costs:	$50
Credits Given:	None
Contact:	Minnesota Governor's Scholars Program
	Minnesota Academic Excellence Foundation
	971 Capitol Square Building, 550 Cedar Street
	St. Paul, MN 55101
	(612) 297-1875; FAX (612) 296-5846

National Endowment for the Humanities Younger Scholars Awards

The Younger Scholars Program provides monetary awards for high school students, enabling the students to conduct independent research and writing projects. Students work closely with their advisers, pursuing a humanities project of interest to the individual student. Studies may be undertaken in any aspect of the humanities such as history, philosophy, language, literature, archaeology, law, ethics, or comparative religion. In the past, Young Scholars have explored various topics: the idea of the modern writer as hero, through an analysis of the work of Aleksandr Solzhenitsyn; the life of Winston Churchill, with attention to Churchill's responses to defeat and failure; and the significance of two major historical female role models of Mexican culture. Students are expected to work full-time on their project during the summer months, meeting at least once a week with their advisers. All projects are expected to result in a substantial research paper that is submitted to the Endowment along with a final narrative report. ***Application deadline: November 1.***

Host School:	The National Endowment for the Humanities (NEH)
Type:	Summer Independent Research and Writing Projects
Location:	At sites chosen by the individual scholar recipients
Duration:	Nine weeks
Dates:	Summer
Qualifications:	Any high school student may apply. Open to United States citizens or foreign nationals who have lived in the United States for at least the preceding three years.
Housing:	At the student's home or arranged by student and adviser at research site.
Costs:	An award of $2,100 is made to the student to cover expenses. $500 of this award is allotted to the student's adviser.
Credits Given:	None
Contact:	National Endowment for the Humanities Younger Scholars Awards
	The National Endowment for the Humanities (NEH)
	Division of Fellowships And Seminars, Room 316
	1100 Pennsylvania Avenue, NW
	Washington, DC 20506

New Jersey Governor's School of the Arts

Talented students who take part in the Governor's School of the Arts at Trenton State have an opportunity to broaden their creative awareness, sharpen their artistic skills, and develop an appreciation of the interrelationships between the arts. Students choose from five curriculum areas. Creative writing students learn to draw from their own experiences and develop their own unique writing style. Music students develop individual skills as well as learn to cooperate and blend their talents through both small- and large-group ensemble work. Students choosing theater take four week-long workshops that focus on mime, vocal training, stage combat, and circus techniques, as well as work on scene and monologue studies throughout the program. Dance students take master classes in ballet, modern and jazz techniques, with special sessions focusing on topics such as warm-up methods, partnering, and choreography. Students talented in the visual arts spend the first two weeks working in a broad variety of media including drawing, design, painting, printmaking, and sculpture. During the second two weeks, students are involved in intensive study in their area of choice. Visiting artists provide performances and demonstrations for the entire school and coach students both individually and in small groups. All students may participate in a multi-arts workshop throughout the session. Trips to dance and theater events, museums, concerts, and planned recreational activities complete this exciting program. ***Application deadline: January 4.***

Host School:	Trenton State College
Type:	Fine and Performing Arts
Location:	Trenton, NJ
Duration:	Four weeks
Dates:	July
Qualifications:	Entering grade 12. Open to New Jersey students gifted in music, dance, theater, creative writing, or visual arts.
Housing:	Participants are housed in dormitories and have meals in the dining halls.
Costs:	None
Credits Given:	None
Contact:	New Jersey Governor's School of the Arts
	Trenton State College
	Trenton, NJ 08650
	(609) 771-3114; FAX (609) 771-3484

Ohio Governor's Gifted Summer Institute

Gifted Summer Institute participants study a theme of their choice through a variety of learning techniques. All students are involved in individual and group projects, and give a student-designed presentation on their last day at the Institute. Course offerings are chosen from a variety of areas. A theater session focuses on improvisations based on social issues of concern to the participants. A Computer-Aided Product Design workshop finds students involved in designing, refining, and testing a product using sophisticated computer design programs. Budding writers might choose the Writing for Performance workshop, which explores the aspects of writing and finds students performing what they have written. A new Internet session helps students to use state-of-the-art techniques to access and utilize a wealth of information. A Great Lakes workshop provides hands-on activities as students explore the properties and problems of the Great Lakes region. Although topics presented may change from year to year, sessions on theater, science, and computers are generally offered. A variety of evening activities including bowling, picnics, pizza parties, and sports complete the program. Applications become available in mid-February. ***Application deadline: April 12.***

Host School: The University of Toledo

Type: Theater, Writing, and Computer-Aided Design Workshops

Location: Toledo, OH

Duration: One week

Dates: Three sessions are held beginning in late June and ending in late July

Qualifications: Entering grades 10 and 11. Open to high-ability Ohio students interested in the topics presented. Applications become available in Mid-February.

Housing: Participants are housed in dormitories and have most meals in the dining halls. Dinners are provided off campus each evening and include picnics as well as restaurant dining. Commuter students are also welcome in special commuter sessions and are provided with lunch.

Costs: $115 per week for residential students; $35 for commuter students. A limited number of need-based scholarships are available.

Credits Given: None

Contact: Dr. Suzanne McFarland
Ohio Governor's Gifted Summer Institute
The University of Toledo
2801 West Bancroft Street
Toledo, OH 43606
(419) 537-4335

Ohio Governor's Summer Institute:
Creative Writing Institutes

Each of the four sessions of this creative writing program held at Bowling Green State University is unique. Two of the sessions offered involve creative writing. The Writer's Summer Workshops present distinguished visiting writers who share skills and techniques with the students. Students also work on their own writing skills through small-group instruction. Other sessions concentrate on broadcast journalism. Recent sessions considered the tension between journalistic ethics and the demand for audience ratings for broadcast news. Another session focused on the trial of Lee Harvey Oswald and the public's perception. Participating students work in a variety of genres, including fiction, poetry, and drama. *Application deadline: April 11.*

Host School:	Bowling Green State University
Type:	Creative Writing and Broadcast Journalism
Location:	Bowling Green, OH
Duration:	One week
Dates:	Four sessions are held from late June through late July
Qualifications:	Entering grades 10 and 11. Open to creative Ohio students interested in the subjects presented each session.
Housing:	Participants are housed in residence halls and have meals in the dining hall.
Costs:	$100. Need-based financial aid is available.
Credits Given:	None
Contact:	Ohio Governor's Summer Institute
	Bowling Green State University
	451 Education Building
	Bowling Green, OH 43403
	(419) 372-7295

Ohio Governor's Summer Institute: Exploring the Arts

Miami University offers a program to students interested in the fine and performing arts. It is designed to stimulate creative thinking, to increase awareness of ideas and concepts, to refine and improve performance skills, and to offer opportunities to present student work to the public. Each of the four sessions focuses on a different aspect of art. Session I, Vocal and Choral Music, offers individual lessons, rehearsals and group performances, along with appearances by guest artists. The Chamber Music Institute, Session II, introduces outstanding high school string, woodwind, and brass players to the various chamber music techniques. Students work in a variety of ensembles and study with professional musicians. Design in Art and Architecture participants explore design in a variety of media during Session III. Students participate in a group design project, visit studios and art museums, and hear invited speakers. Session IV offers a Theater Performance Workshop. Activities include auditioning, improvisation, character and scene work, movement, and television performance. The session concludes with a student performance. Students have access to university facilities including library, theaters, studios, computer labs, ice arena, art museum, and the sports complex. *Application deadline: mid-April.*

Host School:	Miami University
Type:	Fine and Performing Arts
Location:	Oxford, OH
Duration:	One week
Dates:	Four sessions are held beginning in mid-June and running until mid-July.
Qualifications:	Entering grades 10 and 11. Open to Ohio residents interested in one of the arts workshops presented.
Housing:	Participants are housed in dormitories and have meals in the dining hall.
Costs:	$175. Some scholarships are also available.
Credits Given:	None
Contact:	Ohio Governor's Summer Institute
	Miami University
	School of Fine Arts
	112 Hiestand Hall
	Oxford, OH 45056
	(513) 529-6010; FAX (513) 529-1992

Ohio Governor's Summer Institute for Gifted and Talented Students

The Governor's Summer Institute offers motivated students a choice of three interdisciplinary workshops. Session I provides a weeklong experience in African studies. Through various courses and workshops, students seek knowledge and understanding of African history and culture. Session II focuses on the media and studies how reporters gather, organize, and present information in our current age of technology. Students utilize computers in writing their own news stories, learn how a broadcast studio operates, produce their own videos, and explore the manipulation of information and images. Session III participants discover how to tap their potential for school success through use of logic, reasoning, and test-taking skills. Puzzles, brain-teasers, practice tests, and SAT test-taking tips improve students' performance on standardized tests. *Application deadline: April 10.*

Host School:	Central State University
Type:	Workshops on African Studies, the Media, and Test-Taking Skills.
Location:	Wilberforce, OH
Duration:	One week
Dates:	Three sessions are held from late June through mid-July
Qualifications:	Entering grades 10 and 11. Open to Ohio students interested in the sessions offered.
Housing:	Participants are housed in dormitories and have meals in the dining halls.
Costs:	$50
Credits Given:	None
Contact:	Dr. Terrence Glass
	Ohio Governor's Summer Institute for Gifted and Talented Students
	Central State Univetsity
	Department of English and Communication
	212 Wesley Hall
	Wilberforce, OH 45384
	(513) 376-6459

Ohio Summer Institute for Prospective Teachers:
The W. E. B. Du Bois Academy

Minority students have an opportunity to explore the teaching profession and the role of the educator. All students are involved in program-wide activities that include group development and team commitment. These activities are designed to develop leadership and interpersonal skills and examine issues in American education. Students explore what it takes to be an effective teacher. Students choose an area for more intensive study, selecting from a program list that includes Colonies in Space, Science of the City (the geology and ecology of urban environments), the Urban Ethnic Scene, the Arts in the Urban Landscape, and Theater Performance. Additional activities include an exploration of the cultural, political, scientific, artistic, and technological aspects of the Greater Cleveland area. *Application deadline: rolling admissions.*

Host School:	Cleveland State University
Type:	Education
Location:	Cleveland, OH
Duration:	Two weeks
Dates:	Mid-June through beginning of July
Qualifications:	Entering grade 10. Open to gifted and talented Ohio minority students interested in exploring career opportunities in education.
Housing:	Participants are housed in residence halls and have meals in the dining facilities.
Costs:	None
Credits Given:	None
Contact:	Dr. Frank Johns
	Ohio Summer Institute for Prospective Teachers
	Cleveland State University
	College of Education
	Cleveland, OH 44115
	(216) 687-4577; FAX (216) 687-5415

Pennsylvania Governor's School for International Studies

In this unique program, students with a keen interest in global issues study topics that include negotiations and diplomacy, intercultural communications, world geography, and Japanese language and culture. Students choose a major from one of three areas: politics and law, economics and business, and societies and cultures. In these classes, they may analyze how foreign policy is formed, learn the key concepts that guide economic principles and global economy, and debate issues of cultural orientation in an interdependent world. Two small-group Japanese language and culture classes each day provide students with an understanding of Japanese society. Students also work on teams as part of an International Communications and Negotiation Simulation to study and negotiate a set of issues, such as nuclear proliferation, human rights, or global environmental concerns. Leadership, writing, ethics, public speaking, and creative problem solving are stressed across the curriculum. Students also take part in a field trip to Washington, D.C., and are visited by state, national, and international leaders. Cultural, recreational, and social events supplement the academic program. Participants also become eligible for special scholarships at Pennsylvania universities. *Application deadline: February 9.*

Host School:	University of Pittsburgh
Type:	International Studies
Location:	Pittsburgh, PA
Duration:	Five weeks
Dates:	Late June through the end of July
Qualifications:	Entering grade 12. Open to outstanding Pennsylvania students who have a background of foreign language study or second language competency, and who are interested in global issues.
Housing:	Participants are housed in residence halls and have meals in the dining facilities.
Costs:	None
Credits Given:	None
Contact:	Pennsylvania Governor's School for International Studies University of Pittsburgh Pittsburgh, PA Information hotline: (717) 524-5244 or (412) 648-7423

Pennsylvania Governor's School for Teaching

In a program designed to attract bright, creative students to the teaching professions, the program's "school within a school" allows students to learn about the learning process, to use instructional technology and media, and to experience teaching others. Participants are assigned to teams composed of four students of varied backgrounds and interests who work closely with each other and with a faculty mentor. The teams research and plan interdisciplinary activities and work in clusters to develop curricular policy, create schedules, and design the physical plant for a model school. Students get firsthand experience with teaching as each participant researches and develops a lesson plan which will be used to present a lesson to a group of six elementary-level children. The lesson is videotaped, critiqued, and after refining, taught to a different group. Participants explore multicultural issues in education through a walking tour of Lancaster, Pennsylvania, during a festival that emphasizes the student's own heritage, and through leadership workshops. They also experience the latest developments in educational media technology and attend films, seminars, and lectures whose topics include learning styles, educational psychology, learning disabilities, and behaviorism. Leadership and communication workshops, along with recreational, cultural, and social activities, complete the program. *Application deadline: January 19.*

Host School:	Millersville University
Type:	Education
Location:	Millersville, PA
Duration:	Five weeks
Dates:	Early July through mid-August
Qualifications:	Entering grades 11 and 12. Designed for academically talented students interested in the teaching professions and who have been involved in leadership and service activities.
Housing:	Participants are housed in dormitories and have meals in the dining facilities.
Costs:	None
Credits Given:	None
Contact:	Pennsylvania Governor's School for Teaching
	Millersville University
	Millersville, PA
	(717) 871-2026; Information hotline: (717) 524-5244

Pennsylvania Governor's School for the Arts

Students selected for this program major in one area of the creative arts, working intensively on the artistic processes involved in that field. Students also choose a second elective art area to broaden their knowledge of the creative arts. Visual arts majors take design and drawing classes and may work in areas such as sculpture, ceramics, graphic design, animation and video art, and photography. Creative writing majors emphasize either fiction or poetry, focusing on idea development, language usage, criticism, and editing. Dance majors choose ballet, jazz, or modern dance for their major study, but also take intermediate-level classes in the other areas. Students take part in workshops on improvisation, choreography, dance history, and career alternatives, while emphasis is placed on refining and enhancing dance technique. Music majors in instrumental, vocal, and compositional areas take an intensive private lesson each week and also experience small ensemble work, as well as classes in music fundamentals, theory, writing, criticism, and creative studies. Students select a theater major in performance (acting) or technical design and will study acting technique, improvisation, movement and voice. They may also study play analysis, painting, carpentry, and stage management. All students also take part in leadership seminars to help them become active advocates of the arts and participate in recreational activities. *Application deadline: January 18.*

Host School:	Mercyhurst College
Type:	Fine and Performing Arts
Location:	Erie, PA
Duration:	Five weeks
Dates:	Early July through mid-August
Qualifications:	Entering grades 11 and 12. Open to talented students interested in the visual arts (including photography), creative writing, dance, music, or theater.
Housing:	Participants are housed in dormitories and have meals in the dining halls.
Costs:	None
Credits Given:	None
Contact:	Pennsylvania Governor's School for the Arts
	Mercyhurst College
	Erie, PA
	(717) 524-5244

Perspectives

In Perspectives, part of the AEGIS (Academic Enrichment for the Gifted in Summer) program, students consider the rights, responsibilities, and issues faced by voting members of our democratic society. Participants address issues that have no clear or simple answers and must deal with the relationships that exist between these issues. Students are challenged by the connections that exist between the abstract notion of rights and the concrete policies that should be an extension of these rights. Ultimately, it is hoped that students develop a sense of the implications that can be drawn from different positions on different issues. *Contact program director for application information.*

Host School:	Arkansas College
Type:	Public Affairs
Location:	Batesville, AR
Duration:	Three weeks
Dates:	Middle through end of July
Qualifications:	Entering grades 11 and 12. Open to gifted and talented Arkansas students interested in public affairs and politics.
Housing:	Participants are housed in the dormitories and have meals in the dining hall.
Costs:	None
Credits Given:	None
Contact:	Donald Weatherman
	Perspectives
	Arkansas College
	P.O. Box 2317
	Batesville, AR 72503
	(501) 793-9813

Project Pine Forest

Project Pine Forest is a social studies program in which students examine all facets of the development of a pioneer mill town into the "Forestry Capital of the World." Students learn about the wood products industry from seed to finished product and study the economic aspects of the developing industry. Participants plan, design, develop, produce and market new products, take part in simulated negotiations between labor union and management, learn about the industry's ecological impact on the environment, consider the use of natural resources, and predict the future of the town. Recreational activities related to the wood products industry complete this unusual summer simulation. *Application deadline: March 10.*

Host School:	Crossett Public Schools
Type:	Social Studies
Location:	Crossett, AR
Duration:	Two weeks
Dates:	Mid-June
Qualifications:	Entering grades 8 through 10. Open to Arkansas students interested in the environment and the use of natural resources.
Housing:	Participants are housed in the town of Crossett and are provided with meals.
Costs:	None
Credits Given:	None
Contact:	Mary Alice Clinton
	Project Pine Forest
	Crossett Public Schools
	301 West 9th Avenue
	Crossett, AR 71635
	(501) 364-5101; FAX (501) 364-5499

Steps to the Stage

Presented as part of the AEGIS (Academic Enrichment for the Gifted in Summer) program, Steps to the Stage provides creative and talented Arkansas students with the opportunity to explore careers in theater and the performing arts. Participants create a theatrical happening by working together in a collaborative process in all areas of theater development. Performers and designers/technicians engage in monologues, work on scenes, learn about theater design, and paint sets. Through hands-on experiences, students discover how professional theater artists work. The climax of the program is a staged performance featuring both students' performance and design work. ***Contact the program coordinator for application information.***

Host School:	University of the Ozarks
Type:	Theatre and Performing Arts
Location:	Clarksville, AR
Duration:	Three weeks
Dates:	Mid-June through early July
Qualifications:	Entering grades 10 through 12. Open to Arkansas students talented in the arts or theater.
Housing:	Participants are housed in dormitories and have meals in the dining halls.
Costs:	None
Credits Given:	None
Contact:	Patrick Farmer
	Steps to the Stage
	University of the Ozarks
	University Theatre
	Clarksville, AR 72830
	(501) 754-3839

Summer Art Experience

Each summer, the Academy offers 2000 scholarships to high school students to enable both untrained and advanced students to pursue an interest in the visual arts while receiving professional-level art training. The program was designed to provide students with the opportunity to get an overview of the various art disciplines before they need to make educational and career choices. Students may choose one or two classes from offerings that include advertising design, drawing and composition, fashion art, figure drawing, graphic design, interior design, cartooning, motion picture production, photography, product design, sculpture, computer arts, and still-life painting. *Applications are accepted on a first-served basis; apply early.*

Host School:	Academy of Art College
Type:	Visual Arts
Location:	San Francisco, CA
Duration:	Seven weeks
Dates:	Mid-June through early August
Qualifications:	Entering grades 9 through 12. Open to students interested in instruction in the visual arts.
Housing:	Housing is available for students not living in the San Francisco area in the Academy's dormitory or in off-campus apartments.
Costs:	$35 application fee. Students are responsible for their own transportation, fees, and supplies. Residential students have an additional expense for housing and meals.
Credits Given:	None
Contact:	Summer Art Experience
	Academy of Art College
	79 New Montgomery Street
	San Francisco, CA 94105
	(800) 544-ARTS; FAX (415) 546-9737

SummerStage

Arkansas students who have dreamed of careers in professional theater will find this program to be an exciting exploration. Provided as part of the AEGIS (Academic Enrichment for the Gifted in Summer) program, SummerStage provides students with a chance to work with professionals, as a professional, in the performing arts. Talented actors, artists, writers, musicians, singers, and designers all have an opportunity to increase their creative skills while learning and working in a professional theater environment. Workshops presented by working professionals give students a realistic look at careers in the performing arts. In addition to the theatrical work, participants tour professional theater facilities and see live performances. ***Contact the program coordinator for application information.***

Host School:	Harding University
Type:	Theater and Performing Arts Workshop
Location:	Searcy, AR
Duration:	Three weeks
Dates:	Early to end of July
Qualifications:	Entering grades 10 through 12. Open to gifted and talented Arkansas students interested in possible careers in the performing arts.
Housing:	Participants are housed in dormitories and have meals in the dining facilities.
Costs:	None
Credits Given:	None
Contact:	Robin Miller
	Box 895
	SummerStage
	Harding University
	Searcy, AR 72149-0001
	(501) 279-4015

Virginia Governor's School for the Humanities

Students at the Governor's School for the Humanities take part in a broad-based interdisciplinary experience. Students explore the integration of knowledge with the role of the humanities in our future society. Students choose an area of interest for intensive study, selecting from choices that include anthropology/political science, economics/international relations, arts/history, philosophy/literature/music, and arts/humanities. They work in small groups for discussions and study and take part in an interdisciplinary project. An ongoing counseling program, in addition to vocational workshops, provides the students with guidance about education and career opportunities. Recreational, social, cultural, and sports activities complete this intensive summer program. ***Contact program coordinator for application deadline.***

Host School:	University of Richmond
Type:	Humanities
Location:	Richmond, VA
Duration:	Four weeks
Dates:	July
Qualifications:	Entering grades 11 and 12. Open to gifted and talented Virginia students.
Housing:	Participants are housed in the residence halls and have meals in the dining facilities.
Costs:	None
Credits Given:	None
Contact:	Keith Eicher
	Virginia Governor's School for the Humanities
	University of Richmond
	Department of Education
	Richmond, VA 23173
	(804) 289-8431

Student Profile

Jeff Morneau
Vienna, Va.
Virginia Governor's School for the Humanities
Jeff, 17, is a rising senior at James Madison High School.

My tenure at the Virginia Governor's School for the Humanities was the most unique educational experience I've ever had. I didn't know what to expect going in to the program. I only knew that it was a real honor to be accepted. All my teachers had told me about the program. Students who had been before told me I wouldn't ever want it to end. With high hopes and more than a little bit of trepidation, I packed my bags.

My first three days at Governor's School were some of the hardest that I have ever handled. In one fell swoop, I had been taken from the familiar classroom, where I had always been able to manage with relative ease, and thrown amongst some of the brightest people in the state. I had four teachers who all wanted to be there teaching us, and threw themselves into the task. It was a little overwhelming. The program allowed us to choose our main class, the one that we spent four hours a day in. The other class which came later in the day was chosen for us. It was designed to integrate the humanities students with those who were at the Governor's School for the visual and performing arts. Many of my fellow humanities students and I had to adjust and approach subjects in a way that we hadn't ever before.

Over time, and perhaps this was the greatest thing Governor's School taught me, I grew to respect and appreciate different points of view. I didn't leave the program with a complete change in my views, but I am reevaluating some of them. That was just the beginning of the changes the program wrought in me.

I grew more emotionally and intellectually during those four weeks than at any other time in my life. I learned to appreciate people whom I didn't always agree with. I made friends whom I'll never forget. I gained a greater sense of understanding for the world in which I live.

Virginia's Governor's School for the Humanities was an excellent program and is something that I will take lessons from for the rest of my life. My only regret is that more students didn't have the chance to attend and benefit from this program.

Virginia Governor's School for the Visual and Performing Arts

Creatively talented students can explore the techniques, materials, media, and language of the arts and search for the interrelationships between the arts in this extensive, interdisciplinary visual and performing arts program. Small groups of students work together to discuss, study, and take part in an interdisciplinary activity or project. Students work with an artist-in-residence in their own field, but also are encouraged to explore the other artistic disciplines. To increase their understanding of the role of the arts in society, students choose from classes in art history, philosophy, literature, music, patronage and the arts, and arts and the humanities. A counseling component provides students with career and educational guidance, and helps participants discover career opportunities in the arts. Social, recreational, and cultural events complete the program. **_Contact program coordinator for application deadline._**

Host School:	University of Richmond
Type:	Visual and Performing Arts
Location:	Richmond, VA
Duration:	Four weeks
Dates:	July
Qualifications:	Entering grades 11 and 12. Open to gifted and talented Virginia residents interested in an intensive experience in the visual and performing arts.
Housing:	Participants are housed in residence halls and have meals in the dining facilities.
Costs:	None
Credits Given:	None
Contact:	Keith Eicher
	Virginia Governor's School for the Visual and Performing Arts
	University of Richmond
	Department of Education
	Richmond, VA 23173
	(804) 289-8431

$\mathbb{T}$he West Virginia Governor's School for the Arts

Artistically talented West Virginia students can spend an intensive three weeks focusing on four areas of the arts: dance, theater, instrumental music, and the visual arts. Students are taught by renowned performing and teaching artists serving as role models and mentors while sharing their skills with students. During the morning, each student participates in an intensive class in the field of his or her choice. Afternoon classes are interdisciplinary in nature and designed to foster an appreciation of how a specific area of art fits into the role of all of the arts in our society. Late afternoons are filled with practice time and recreational activities. Numerous field trips including a trip to the Pittsburgh Art Museum and to the theater are part of the program. Evening cultural activities such as concerts, poetry readings, performances, and guest speakers round out these exciting three weeks. To help students get a realistic look at life as a practicing artist, guest artists meet with small groups of students to discuss career paths and options. *Application deadline: February 15.*

Host School:	Fairmont State College
Type:	Fine and Performing Arts
Location:	Fairmont, WV
Duration:	Three weeks
Dates:	Late June through mid-July
Qualifications:	Entering grade 11. Open to creatively talented West Virginia students who are selected through local, regional, and state level auditions.
Housing:	Participants are housed in a dormitory and have meals in the dining hall.
Costs:	None
Credits Given:	None
Contact:	Dr. Virginia Simmons
	The West Virginia Governor's School for the Arts
	West Virginia Department of Education
	Building 6, Room 362, Capitol Complex
	Charleston, WV 25305-0330
	(304) 558-0160; FAX (304) 558-0048

Western Maryland Writing Center

The Playwriting and Bookwriting Workshops seek out creative young people for cooperative learning. The Playwriting Workshop provides students with the opportunity to be a playwright, producer, director, and star of their own play. These cooperative learning groups write their own plays, designing the sets, costumes, and props needed for final production. Each group chooses to present their creation as a radio play, video, or live performance. A visit to the Cumberland Summer Theater helps students learn about staging. The week culminates with a Dinner Theater Evening for parents and guests. The Bookwriting Workshop guides and directs students in the step-by-step process of writing and illustrating a book. Students are introduced to the components of a story, developing their own ideas into a book-length manuscript. The young authors then use their creative minds to develop original illustrations for their work, and bind the finished product into a hardbound book. The program also features an Author's Reception for parents and guests. *Application deadline: April 21.*

Host School:	Frostburg State University
Type:	Book and Playwriting Workshops
Location:	Frostburg, MD
Duration:	One week
Dates:	Two sessions are held in mid-July
Qualifications:	Entering grades 5 and 6. These programs are open to students interested in writing and eager to create their own play or book.
Housing:	Students are housed in the dormitories and have meals in the dining hall.
Costs:	$200. Need-based financial aid is available.
Credits Given:	None
Contact:	John Festerman
	Western Maryland Writing Center
	Board of Education of Allegany County
	108 Washington Street, P.O. Box 1724
	Cumberland, MD 21502
	(301) 759-2014

Science/Math/Technology

Academically Interested Minorities (AIM)

The AIM program is designed to help minority students make a smooth transition from high school to college. The program targets students interested in the careers of science, engineering, or management. Students enroll in college-level classes, arranged in a pattern similar to that found at many colleges, in math, computer science, communications, humanities, and chemistry. Tutoring periods are included in the schedule to provide students with the tools needed to succeed in college. Fridays are reserved for career institutes in which students work with professional engineers or administrators. The career institute helps students learn about career options and how to set and achieve professional goals. Tours are also arranged as part of the career awareness activities. Evening social events complement the academic program. *Application deadline: March 31.*

Host School:	GMI Engineering and Management Institute
Type:	Science and Engineering
Location:	Flint, MI
Duration:	Six weeks
Dates:	Mid-July through late August
Qualifications:	Entering grade 12. Open to minority students. Applicants must have at least a 3.0 grade point average in high school math, chemistry, and English classes, and have taken the equivalent of algebra I and II and geometry, chemistry (with lab), and two years of English.
Housing:	Participants are housed in the dormitories of GMI Engineering and Management Institute. Meals are provided.
Costs:	None
Credits Given:	None
Contact:	Ricky D. Brown
	Academically Interested Minorities
	GMI Engineering and Management Institute
	1700 West Third Avenue
	Flint, MI 48504-4898
	(313) 762-9825 or (800) 955-4464 ext. 9825; FAX (810) 762-9807

Advanced Chemistry Applications Program

Each student in this program takes at least one class in chemistry or a related discipline while being actively involved in research with a university faculty member. Students may choose from several possible areas of research. Past research options have included studies in the free radical reactions of organic compounds, the synthesis and reactions of substituted aromatic compounds, and a study of alkali metal tellurides in liquid ammonia solutions. Through close association with a practicing scientist, participants develop a realistic view of life as a scientist, as well as deriving benefits from the student-mentor relationship. Students may choose to participate in the program for either one or both sessions and will receive a scholarship. Students may receive a part-time salary for their work. ***Application deadline: April 1.***

Host School:	Tarleton State University
Type:	Chemistry Study and Internship
Location:	Stephenville, TX
Duration:	Five to ten weeks
Dates:	Two five-week sessions are held. Session I: June through the first week in July; Session II: Early July through mid-August.
Qualifications:	Entering grade 12. Students should be at least 16 years old by May 31, and be interested in chemistry or a related field. Applicants should have combined SAT scores of at least 1100, an ACT score of at least 24, or equivalent PSAT scores.
Housing:	Participants are housed in the residence halls and have meals in the dining facilities.
Costs:	Students receive scholarships toward college course fees. Students may receive a part-time salary for their research work.
Credits Given:	College credits are awarded. Number awarded depends upon courses chosen.
Contact:	Advanced Chemistry Applications Program
	Tarleton State University
	Department of Physical Sciences
	Box T-69, Tarleton Station
	Stephenville, TX 76402
	(817) 968-9143

Aerospace—The Final Frontier

Aerospace—The Final Frontier is presented for Arkansas students as part of the AEGIS (Academic Enrichment for the Gifted in Summer) program. Aerospace students learn the basic principles of flight in the classroom and then utilize these principles through hands-on experiences. The students design and build hot-air balloons, kites, airplanes, and rockets to test and improve their own theoretical understanding. Through interaction with the professional staff and with other aviation experts, participants gain an understanding of the impact that aviation and space have on life in modern society, as well as learn about career opportunities in the aerospace industries. *Contact the program coordinator for application deadline.*

Host School:	Crowley's Ridge ESC
Type:	Aerospace
Location:	Harrisburg, AR
Duration:	Two weeks
Dates:	Mid-July
Qualifications:	Entering grades 10 through 12. Open to Arkansas students interested in flight.
Housing:	Participants are housed in the dormitories and have meals in the dining hall.
Costs:	None
Credits Given:	None
Contact:	Louis Midkiff
	Aerospace—The Final Frontier
	Crowley's Ridge ESC
	P.O. Box 377
	Harrisburg, AR 72432
	(501) 578-5426

American Indian Biological and Computer Sciences

The Biological and Computer Sciences Workshop is designed to introduce young American Indian students to the richness of a college education. Students explore the worlds of biology or computer science every morning, and investigate a variety of other topics each afternoon. Here is a chance to investigate possible careers in the sciences, engineering, or technology through interaction with professional role models. Students develop an awareness of college life, celebrate American Indian culture, and meet motivated young people from all over Michigan. Participants come away from the program with an understanding of postsecondary educational opportunities. Sports and recreational activities including swimming, movies, and ball games complete this exciting program. *Application deadline: May 1.*

Host School:	Michigan Technological University
Type:	Biology and Computer Science
Location:	Houghton, MI
Duration:	One week
Dates:	Early June
Qualifications:	Entering grades 7 through 9. The program is open to American Indian students.
Housing:	Students are housed in the dormitories and have meals in the dining hall.
Costs:	No cost to Michigan residents. Out-of-state students will be expected to pay for the cost of the program, food, and lodging.
Credits Given:	None
Contact:	Ms. Kerry Hicks
	American Indian Biological and Computer Sciences Workshop
	Michigan Technological University
	Youth Programs Office
	1400 Townsend Drive
	Houghton, MI 49931
	(906) 487-2219; FAX (906) 487-3101

American Indian Research Opportunities (AIRO) Programs

The American Indian Research Opportunities (AIRO) Program offers several summer enrichment programs targeting American Indian youth. These programs seek to promote the students' interest in the sciences, engineering, and mathematics, encouraging them to explore careers in these fields. The Minority Research Apprenticeship (MAP) program exposes high school juniors and seniors to meaningful work experiences in scientific research laboratories, targeting the biomedical and agricultural areas. In addition to laboratory work, the program helps participants improve their mathematical, writing, and communication skills in preparation for college enrollment. An additional program, the American Indians in Mathematics Project, is designed to increase the participation and success of first-generation, college-bound American Indian students in mathematics-based curricula. This program targets student leaders from grades 9 and 10, and includes a follow-up program after the summer experience. *Contact the AIRO office for more information about these and other programs.*

Host School: Montana State University
Type: Science and Mathematics Research and Study Programs
Location: Bozeman, MT
Duration: Two to six weeks
Dates: Selected dates in July and August
Qualifications: Entering grades 9 through 12. These programs are directed to American Indian students interested in science and/or mathematics. Some programs are open to members of other minority groups traditionally underrepresented in the sciences and engineering.
Housing: Students are housed in the dormitories and have meals in the dining hall.
Costs: Most programs are provided without cost to the participants. Minority Apprenticeship Program (MAP) participants are paid $4.50 per hour for their work, but are responsible for the cost of their weekend meals.
Credits Given: None
Contact: Dr. David Young
American Indian Research Opportunities (AIRO) Programs
Montana State University
309 Culbertson Hall
Bozeman, MT 59717
(406) 994-5567; FAX (406) 994-5559

American Indian Science and Engineering Society Science Camp (AISES) Clarkson Mathematics Program

Sponsored by AISES (the American Indian Science and Engineering Society) and Clarkson University, the program seeks to develop the participant's interest in mathematics through a creative, hands-on approach. The program strives to strengthen students' problem-solving and performance skills, and to increase their awareness of career opportunities in the fields of science and engineering. Instruction in science, mathematics, and computer science is combined with a personal development program (Vision). Students interact with American Indian role models involved in scientific professions and participate in field trips during the program. Recreational activities are planned for each day. ***Application deadline: mid-February.***

Host School:	Clarkson University
Type:	Mathematics, Engineering, and Computer Science
Location:	Potsdam, NY
Duration:	Four weeks
Dates:	Month of July
Qualifications:	Entering grade 11. Open to American Indian students interested in science and mathematics who are in the top half of their class.
Housing:	Participants are housed in a dormitory and have meals in the dining hall.
Costs:	None
Credits Given:	None
Contact:	Mathematics Program for Native Americans
	AISES
	1630 30th Street, Suite 301
	Boulder, CO 80301
	(303) 939-0023

Artificial Intelligence—A Knowledge-Based Approach

Middle school students interested in computer science can learn about computers and artificial intelligence in this program presented as part of the AEGIS (Academic Enrichment for the Gifted in Summer) program. Students attempt to find answers to questions like, Can computers learn? Can computers imitate human behavior? Participants use the MicroVax 3600 system while exploring areas that include knowledge representation, pattern matching, problem solving, natural language processing, and expert systems. A full array of recreational activities completes this program. ***Contact program coordinator for application deadline.***

Host School:	Harding University
Type:	Computer Science
Location:	Searcy, AR
Duration:	Two weeks
Dates:	Late June through mid-July
Qualifications:	Entering grade 8. Open to Arkansas students interested in computer science.
Housing:	Participants are housed in the dormitories and have meals in the dining hall.
Costs:	None
Credits Given:	None
Contact:	Travis Thompson
	Artificial Intelligence—A Knowledge-Based Approach
	Harding University
	Box 934
	Searcy, AR 72149-0001
	(501) 279-4464

Arts and Sciences at Adrian College
Science Focus: Environmental Sciences

Students interested in one of the disciplines of science, such as biology, ecology, or chemistry, can investigate the effects of human use and its impact on the environment from the perspective of their discipline. Each participant chooses an area of focus from topics including environmental journalism, animal behavior, environmental chemistry, archaeology, cultural anthropology, and freshwater ecology. Students seek solutions to environmental problems such as the destruction of the natural wetlands. Discussion groups, hands-on lab and field experiences, research trips, simulations, and speakers all combine to provide a new perspective on environmental concerns. Recreational activities are planned. *Application deadline: February 28. Apply through your high school guidance office.*

Host School:	Adrian College
Type:	Environmental science
Location:	Adrian, MI
Duration:	Two weeks
Dates:	End of June through mid-July
Qualifications:	Entering grades 11 and 12. Open to current Michigan public and private school students.
Housing:	Participants are housed in the residence halls and have meals in the dining facilities.
Costs:	$200. Need-based scholarship aid is available.
Credits Given:	None
Contact:	Dr. James Borland
	Arts and Sciences at Adrian College
	Adrian College
	110 South Madison Street
	Adrian, MI 49221
	(517) 265-5161

Careers in Applied Science and Technology (CAST)

The Careers in Applied Science and Technology (CAST) program is designed to expose participants to the human side of science and technology. Two central workshops stress the connections between science and life. "Presenting Specialized Information" helps students improve their communication skills, and "Science, Technology, and Society" explores the interrelationships between technical and social issues. Two-week tracks allow participants to increase their laboratory research or science writing skills. A series of visits to state-of-the-art laboratories and meetings with scientists in the field broaden students' understanding of research and its place in modern life. Students spend about half their program time engaged in group projects, choosing either a project to design, write, and produce a science and technology classroom magazine, or a team research project in a renowned research center on campus. CAST members also have access to all other extracurricular activities presented for pre-college students, including sports, social, and college admissions workshops. *Application deadline: April 15.*

Host School:	Carnegie Mellon University
Type:	Science and Technology
Location:	Pittsburgh, PA
Duration:	Six weeks
Dates:	Late June through early August
Qualifications:	Entering grades 11 and 12. Open to students interested in exploring possible careers in applied science and technology.
Housing:	Participants are housed in the residence halls. The dining plan provides 19 meals per week.
Costs:	None
Credits Given:	None
Contact:	Careers in Applied Science and Technology (CAST)
	Carnegie Mellon University
	Pre-College Programs
	5000 Forbes Avenue
	Pittsburgh, PA 15213-3890
	(412) 268-2082; FAX (412) 268-7838

Chemical Engineering Summer Workshop

The Chemical Engineering Summer Workshop provides participants with exposure to all of the engineering disciplines while focusing on chemical engineering. The program introduces participants to the field of chemical engineering through a study of mathematics, chemistry, and physics, and gives students a close look at engineering applications and career opportunities. Field trips are scheduled to area industrial and research sites, a nuclear power plant, a candy factory, a foundry, and an art museum to view the process of art restorations. Laboratory research, computer use and applications, creative problem solving, as well as independent research projects complete the program. Students also have access to the university's extensive recreational and sports facilities. *Application deadline: March 30.*

Host School:	University of Toledo
Type:	Chemical Engineering
Location:	Toledo, OH
Duration:	Three weeks
Dates:	Early July through late July
Qualifications:	Entering grades 11 and 12. Open to high-achieving students interested in exploring careers in chemical engineering. Participation is limited to United States citizens.
Housing:	Participants are housed in the dormitories and have meals in the dining facilities.
Costs:	None. Students are paid a stipend of $200; this may be used to offset incidental personal expenses and transportation to and from the program.
Credits Given:	None
Contact:	Mrs. Gale Mentzer
	Chemical Engineering Summer Workshop
	University of Toledo
	Academic Coordinator
	Department of Chemical Engineering
	Toledo, OH 43606
	(419) 537-4400

Cornell Environmental Sciences Interns Program (CESIP)

Students interested in the environmental sciences are encouraged to pursue research careers through their experiences in the Cornell Environmental Sciences Interns Program (CESIP). The program begins with a weeklong orientation to environmental science at Cornell's Arnot Research Forest and then continues with five weeks on campus. During the on-campus portion, each intern participates in a field or laboratory-based research project, working on the project three days each week. At the conclusion of the program, the intern presents a summary of research results to his or her peers. On nonresearch days, the interns work with elementary students at Ithaca schools, presenting environmental science lessons. Additional activities include career exploration through interviews and meetings with environmental professionals, as well as career counseling to help with academic and vocational planning. Students also participate in weekly seminars that consider the role of ethics in science. CESIP participants are provided with a wide range of recreational and cultural activities that fill the evening and weekend time. *Application deadline: April 1.*

Host School:	Cornell University
Type:	Environmental Science Internship
Location:	Ithaca, NY
Duration:	Six weeks
Dates:	Late June through early August
Qualifications:	Entering grade 12. Open to New York State students interested in environmental science. Admission is highly selective.
Housing:	Participants are housed in the dormitories with over 800 high school students enrolled in the Cornell Summer College. Meals are provided in the dining halls.
Costs:	None. Room, board, and a small stipend are provided for all participants.
Credits Given:	None
Contact:	Cornell Environmental Sciences Interns Program (CESIP)
	Cornell University
	Department of Natural Resources
	108 Fernow Hall
	Ithaca, NY 14853-3001
	(607) 255-2814; FAX (607) 255-2815

Discovery

Discovery is an enrichment and apprenticeship program designed to introduce participants to career opportunities in science and technology. The program consists of an intensive summer session with academic year follow-up. The academic component includes classroom instruction in mathematics and English, with extensive use of computers and instruction in scientific research methodology. In the apprenticeship, students get hands-on experience in the laboratory and field, learning lab techniques under the guidance of a faculty sponsor and gaining firsthand knowledge about what a scientist does. The areas of study include animal science, plant pathology, environmental science, ceramic engineering, marine and coastal science, and food science, among others. Workshops on career exploration and time management complete the program. *Application deadline: March 5.*

Host School:	Rutgers University, Cook College
Type:	Science Study and Internship
Location:	New Brunswick, NJ
Duration:	Five weeks
Dates:	Mid-July to mid-August
Qualifications:	Entering grades 11 and 12. Open to New Jersey resident minority students interested in the life and physical sciences. Students should rank in the top third of their high school class or have demonstrated academic potential.
Housing:	Participants are housed in the residence halls and have meals in the dining halls.
Costs:	Some fees will be assessed, but costs have not been determined at this time.
Credits Given:	Three college credits Discovery
Contact:	Rutgers University, Cook College Martin Hall, Room 109-B P.O. Box 231 New Brunswick, NJ 08903-0231 (908) 932-9650; FAX (908) 932-8880

Department of Energy High School Honors Program in Ecology

The United States Department of Energy (DOE) in conjunction with Pacific Northwest Laboratory (PNL) offers students the unique opportunity to study a wide range of ecosystems, including ocean, desert, forest, river, and stream, that span the state of Washington. Students should be interested in discovering how ecosystems function, interrelate, and change. This program emphasizes physically intensive field experiences, and participants need to be able to work in a variety of terrains. Combining field study with advanced satellite technology, students study biology, chemistry, computer science and math. PNL scientists also present seminars on topics such as food irradiation, robotics, and molecular biology. **Application deadline: Contact program or State Department of Education for information.**

Host School:	Pacific Northwest Laboratory
Type:	Ecology Internship
Location:	Sites in Washington State
Duration:	Two weeks
Dates:	Beginning to mid-August
Qualifications:	Entering grade 12 and first year of college. Open to students who have demonstrated superior academic achievement and have received recognition in science. Participants should be United States citizens. A background in field biology or chemistry is desirable. Students are selected by State Departments of Education, one student per state.
Housing:	Participants are housed in approved facilities arranged by the Laboratory and have meals provided.
Costs:	None. All expenses, including transportation to and from the Laboratory, are provided.
Credits Given:	None
Contact:	DOE High School Honors Program in Ecology Pacific Northwest Laboratory ER–80 United States Department of Energy Washington, DC 20585 (202) 586-8949

Department of Energy High School Honors Program in Environmental Science

Sponsored by the United States Department of Energy (DOE) and the Oak Ridge National Laboratory (ORNL), this program's theme is identifying and solving environmental problems caused by conventional energy technologies. Studies focus on the analysis of aquatic and terrestrial ecosystems. At ORNL, interdisciplinary teams of researchers work together at one of the world's largest environmental research laboratories. The student participants form research teams and join scientists in the investigation of environmental issues and problems. Students also attend lectures, visit laboratories and take part in field trips. *Application deadline: Contact program or State Department of Education for information.*

Host School:	Oak Ridge National Laboratory
Type:	Environmental Science Internship
Location:	Oak Ridge, TN
Duration:	Two weeks
Dates:	Middle through late July
Qualifications:	Entering grade 12. Open to students who have demonstrated superior academic achievement and have received recognition in science. Students should have completed biology and chemistry; course work in environmental science, geology, or advanced life sciences desirable. United States citizens only. Interns are selected by individual State Departments of Education.
Housing:	Participants are housed in approved facilities arranged by the Laboratory and are provided with meals.
Costs:	All expenses, including transportation for the student to and from the facility, are paid by the sponsoring agencies.
Credits Given:	None
Contact:	DOE High School Honors Program in Environmental Science Oak Ridge National Laboratory ER–80 United States Department of Energy Washington, DC 20585 (202) 586-8949

Department of Energy High School Honors Program in Materials Science

Sponsored by the United States Department of Energy (DOE) and Argonne National Laboratory, the program provides high school students with hands-on experience in ceramics and superconductivity. Activities are designed to develop curiosity, expose students to a research atmosphere, and provide interaction with scientists and peers. Lectures and demonstrations focus on current and potential applications of superconducting ceramics in basic science, engineering, electronics, and medical research. Students have access to the libraries of the Laboratory. Each student participant is expected to prepare a short paper on possible uses of superconductivity, give an oral presentation, and demonstrate an understanding of the principles of superconductivity. ***Application deadline: Contact program or State Department of Education for information.***

Host School:	Argonne National Laboratory
Type:	Materials Science Internship
Location:	Argonne, IL
Duration:	Two weeks
Dates:	Middle to late June
Qualifications:	Entering grade 12 or first year of college. Students should have demonstrated superior academic achievement and have received recognition in science. Completion of course work in biology, chemistry, and physics is preferable. One student from each state will be selected for this program. Contact individual State Departments of Education for information.
Housing:	Participants are housed at a nearby college. Meals are provided.
Costs:	None. All expenses including transportation for the student to and from the Laboratory are provided.
Credits Given:	None
Contact:	DOE High School Honors Program in Materials Science
	Argonne National Laboratory
	ER–80
	United States Department of Energy
	Washington, DC 20585
	(202) 586-8949

Department of Energy High School Honors Research Program at the National Synchrotron Light Source (NSLS)

Sponsored by the United States Department of Energy (DOE) and a host laboratory, this unique program gives high school students an opportunity to work at a state-of-the-art research facility. The major theme of this program is the study of basic and applied research in physical and life sciences. Current research at NSLS includes investigations in biology (protein structure), technology (photo etching), chemistry (photoemission spectroscopy), physics (surface structures), and other disciplines. Students attend lectures, visit laboratories, and interact with lab scientists and engineers. They also perform several experiments on NSLS beam lines, the world's brightest source of X rays and vacuum ultraviolet radiation. Written laboratory reports and oral presentations are required. *Application deadline: Contact program or State Department of Education for information.*

Host School:	Brookhaven National Laboratory
Type:	Physical and Life Sciences Internship
Location:	Upton, NY
Duration:	Two weeks
Dates:	Late July through early August
Qualifications:	Entering grade 12. Students must demonstrate superior academic achievement and recognition in science and/or math. Advanced placement classes in physics, chemistry, and/or biology are desirable. One student from each state is selected. Contact State Department of Education for information.
Housing:	Students are housed in approved facilities arranged by the Laboratory.
Costs:	None. All expenses are paid by the sponsoring agencies including transportation to and from the facility.
Credits Given:	None
Contact:	DOE High School Honors Research Program at the National Synchrotron Light Source
	Brookhaven National Laboratory
	ER–80
	United States Department of Energy
	Washington, DC 20585
	(202) 586-8949

Department of Energy High School Honors Research Program in Particle Physics

Sponsored by the United States Department of Energy (DOE) and the Fermi Accelerator Laboratory, this program gives 58 high school students the opportunity to interact with physicists and graduate students at a state-of-the-art scientific research center. The facility is a proton accelerator which provides the ability to carry out research in high-energy particle physics. Student participants join groups of researchers from the United States and around the world, doing frontier research on the properties of elementary particles and using the world's highest energy particle accelerator. *Application deadline: Contact program or State Department of Education for information.*

Host School:	Fermi National Accelerator Laboratory
Type:	Physics Internship
Location:	Chicago, IL
Duration:	Two weeks
Dates:	Middle through late June
Qualifications:	Entering grade 12 or first year of college. Students must show superior academic achievement and recognition in science and/or mathematics. They should have completed at least one year each of physics and calculus and have some knowledge of computers. Students selected by State Departments of Education, one per state.
Housing:	Students are housed in approved facilities arranged by the Laboratory.
Costs:	None. All expenses are paid by the sponsoring agencies, including transportation for the student to and from the facility.
Credits Given:	None
Contact:	DOE High School Honors Research Program in Particle Physics
	Fermi National Accelerator Laboratory
	ER–80
	United States Department of Energy
	Washington, DC 20585
	(202) 586-8949

Department of Energy High School Life Sciences Honors Program

Sponsored by the United States Department of Energy (DOE) and the Lawrence Berkeley Laboratory, this program offers summer research opportunities for outstanding high school students interested in the life sciences. Participants are associated with members of the scientific staff in an intensive two-week training program designed to provide research experience in biomedical research, biotechnology, chemical biodynamics, and biology. The program also features lectures by scientists, including Nobel laureates; tutorial instruction; tours of the University of California, Berkeley, and use of its library; and access to the facilities of the Laboratory. ***Application deadline: Contact State Department of Education for information.***

Host School:	Lawrence Berkeley Laboratory
Type:	Scientific Research Internship
Location:	Berkeley, CA
Duration:	Two weeks
Dates:	Late July through early August
Qualifications:	Entering grade 12 or first year of college. Students must demonstrate superior academic achievement and recognition in the sciences. Completion of advanced classes in the life sciences and chemistry is helpful. One student from each state is selected for this program. Contact individual State Department of Education for information.
Housing:	Students are housed in approved facilities arranged by the Laboratory.
Costs:	None. All expenses are paid by the sponsoring agencies including transportation for the student to and from the Laboratory.
Credits Given:	None
Contact:	DOE High School Life Sciences Honors Program
	Lawrence Berkeley Laboratory
	ER–80
	United States Department of Energy
	Washington, DC 20585
	(202) 586-8949

Department of Energy High School Supercomputer Honors Program

Sponsored by the United States Department of Energy (DOE) and a host laboratory, this program gives high school students firsthand experience working in a state-of-the-art research facility and interacting with research scientists. High school students selected for this program get hands-on experience using the world's fastest and most sophisticated computers at the Lawrence Livermore Laboratory's National Magnetic Fusion Energy Center. The program seeks to encourage students to regard supercomputers as research tools and to motivate them to study computer science. Students solve problems in mathematics, physics, and computer graphics. Each student is also expected to complete a programming project that demonstrates the capacities of supercomputers. *Application deadline: Contact program or State Department of Education for information.*

Host School:	Lawrence Livermore National Laboratory
Type:	Computer Science Internship
Location:	Livermore, CA
Duration:	Two weeks
Dates:	Middle to end of June
Qualifications:	Entering grade 12 or first year of college. Students must demonstrate superior academic achievement and have received recognition in science and/or mathematics, be computer literate, and United States citizens. One student is selected from each state.
Housing:	Participants are housed in approved facilities arranged by the Laboratory. Meals are provided.
Costs:	None. All expenses, including transportation for the student to and from the facility, are provided.
Credits Given:	None
Contact:	DOE High School Supercomputer Honors Program
	Lawrence Livermore National Laboratory
	ER–80
	United States Department of Energy
	Washington, DC 20585
	(202) 586-8949

Engineering Career Orientation (ECO)

The Engineering Career Orientation (ECO) program seeks to stimulate interest in careers in science and engineering among minority students and to provide practical hands-on experiences in academic areas related to these fields. Students take four hour-long classes each day in such subjects as precalculus, chemistry, introduction to computers, and writing. The two-week session is a shortened version of the four-week program; it provides an introduction to science and engineering careers. One of the goals of the program is to teach students how to learn. Evening presentations by minority representatives from private industry and university personnel provide role models for the students while familiarizing them with opportunities for careers in the engineering disciplines. Friday field trips bring students to area engineering facilities to acquaint them with engineering concepts and their applications. Recreational field trips complete the summer experience. Cash prizes are awarded to outstanding students at the conclusion of the program. *Application deadline: May 15.*

Host School:	University of Massachusetts
Type:	Engineering
Location:	Amherst, MA
Duration:	Two to four weeks
Dates:	July
Qualifications:	Entering grades 9 through 12. Open to minority students (Black, Hispanic, and Native American) who are United States citizens. Students should be interested in possible careers in science, engineering, or math and have demonstrated high potential.
Housing:	Participants are housed in the residence halls and have meals in the dining facilities.
Costs:	Fees vary from year to year depending upon program length and funding. The four-week program generally costs about $750; in past years, the two-week program has been free. Financial aid is available.
Credits Given:	None
Contact:	Engineering Career Orientation
	University of Massachusetts
	Minority Engineering Program
	128 Marston Hall
	Amherst, MA 01003
	(413) 545-2030

The Engineering Experience for Minorities: TEEM

The Engineering Experience for Minorities (TEEM) introduces minority students to opportunities available in the field of engineering while exposing them to the intellectual challenges found in college-level study. The program includes academic study through laboratory activities, computer work, library research, and engineering projects. Students solve real problems using the methods of practicing engineers. Computer sessions focus on basic skills and computer graphics. Laboratory tours and informational discussions with engineers and educators provide a look at opportunities in engineering today. College planning workshops are also part of the program. An additional feature of this program is its emphasis on improving communication as a necessary skill for professional success. Sports and recreational activities are planned. *Application deadline: March 31.*

Host School:	Rutgers University
Type:	Engineering
Location:	Piscataway, NJ
Duration:	Three weeks
Dates:	Middle through end of July
Qualifications:	Entering grade 12. Open to Black, Hispanic, and Native American residents of New Jersey. Students should be interested in exploring career options in engineering.
Housing:	Participants are housed in residence halls and have meals in the dining facilities.
Costs:	None
Credits Given:	None
Contact:	Ms. Ilene Rosen
	The Engineering Experience for Minorities
	Rutgers University
	College of Engineering, Room B-110
	P.O. Box 909
	Piscataway, NJ 08855-0909
	(908) 445-2687; FAX (908) 445-5878

Engineering Summer Residency Program (ESRP)

This program seeks to introduce students to the world of engineering and to career opportunities in this field. The daily schedule is similar to that of college students and includes lectures, laboratories, demonstrations, and a field trip. Computer science, as well as engineering activities, are explored. Through this program, it is hoped that the participants discover how the sciences, math, computer knowledge, and English are all important tools of the professional engineer. Students are also encouraged to learn about the academic preparations they should make if they wish to become engineers. Students get a taste of college life, as well as an opportunity to interact with University of California, Davis, faculty, engineering students, and professionals in the field. Evenings are filled with group projects, recreational, and social activities. ***Application deadline: April 1.***

Host School:	University of California, Davis
Type:	Engineering and Computer Science
Location:	Davis, CA
Duration:	One week
Dates:	Late June
Qualifications:	Entering grades 11 and 12. Open to population groups that traditionally have had limited representation in engineering (women, minorities, the disadvantaged). The program is designed for students interested in learning about possible career opportunities in the field of engineering.
Housing:	Participants are housed in the dormitories and have meals in the dining halls.
Costs:	None
Credits Given:	None
Contact:	Engineering Summer Residency Program
	University of California, Davis
	Dean's Office, College of Engineering
	1050 E Engineering II
	Davis, CA 95616
	(916) 752-3316

Exploring the Geosciences: Earth, Atmosphere, and Environment

Student participants have a unique opportunity to explore Oklahoma as seen through the eyes of three scientific disciplines: geology/geophysics, geography, and meteorology. Students take field trips to the Arbuckle and Wichita Mountains to collect geological samples for sectioning and examining specimens in the laboratories. Studies involving tornadoes, lightning, hail, and climate changes, along with trips to the National Severe Storms Lab and the National Weather Service Forecast Office, aid in an understanding of Oklahoma's weather. The field of geography is explored through satellite images, air photos, and maps, as well as field surveying. Special activities and events are planned for the evenings and weekends. Separate academies are held for upper- and lower-level students. *Application deadline: April 1.*

Host School:	University of Oklahoma
Type:	Earth Science
Location:	Norman, OK
Duration:	Three weeks for students in grades 11 and 12; two weeks for students grades 9 and 10.
Dates:	Middle through late July
Qualifications:	Entering grades 9 through 12. Open to Oklahoma residents interested in science and mathematics.
Housing:	Participants are housed in a residence hall. An all-you-can-eat meal plan is provided at the university cafeteria.
Costs:	None
Credits Given:	None
Contact:	Exploring the Geosciences
	University of Oklahoma
	Precollegiate Programs: Summer Academy
	1700 Asp Avenue
	Norman, OK 73037-0001
	(405) 325-6897; FAX (405) 325-7679

Field Studies in Multidisciplinary Biology

Students who participate in this summer academy program have an opportunity to study and research organisms in their natural environment. Monday through Friday, participants live and work at the Biological Station on Lake Texoma. There they learn to classify organisms and study the grasses, plants, trees, insects, fish, reptiles, birds, and mammals found in Oklahoma. The goal of the program is to aid students in developing investigative laboratory and communication skills. The program provides learning experiences that cannot be found in the students' home schools. Adult supervision is provided for students who choose to remain at the Biological Station over the weekends. This is a fast-paced, intensive program requiring commitment from the participants. ***Application deadline: April 1.***

Host School:	University of Oklahoma
Type:	Field Biology
Location:	Norman, OK
Duration:	Four weeks
Dates:	Mid-June through early July
Qualifications:	Entering grades 11 and 12. Open to Oklahoma residents who demonstrate above-average interest in science and mathematics. Selection is competitive.
Housing:	Participants are housed in the Biological Station residence hall and have meals in the cafeteria. Weekend residence is optional; supervision is provided for students who choose to remain at the Biological Station over the weekends.
Costs:	None. A small stipend given at the end of the program to help defray incidental personal expenses.
Credits Given:	None
Contact:	Field Studies in Multidisciplinary Biology
	University of Oklahoma
	Precollegiate Programs: Summer Academy
	1700 Asp Avenue
	Norman, OK 73037-0001
	(405) 325-6897

FOCUS Program in Mathematics and Science

The FOCUS program seeks to encourage talented multicultural high school freshmen to work toward careers in mathematics and the sciences. This is a three-year summer program that builds upon the students' high school studies, and prepares them for rigorous college programs. During the first summer, FOCUS One, students are introduced to a series of practical problems in science, and participate in hands-on activities and discussions to find solutions. Students also study the ways in which mathematics and the computer sciences support scientific research. Writing skills are addressed through work on laboratory reports. The second summer, FOCUS Two, explores the history of the universe. Once again, math, computer science, and writing skills are used to complement the scientific studies. Students discover the interrelationships of the various sciences including physics, chemistry, geology, and biology. Summer FOCUS Three introduces students to college-level study through a college credit course. Throughout the three years, students learn about college planning, admissions, and financial aid. A new class of FOCUS students is chosen every other year. ***Contact program coordinator for application deadline.***

Host School:	Dickinson College
Type:	Mathematics and Science
Location:	Carlisle, PA
Duration:	Three weeks during each of three summers
Dates:	Mid-June through early July
Qualifications:	Students apply to the program while in grade 9 and attend during the summers before grades 10 and 11. Students successful in the first two summers are invited to take a 3-credit college course during the summer before their senior year. The program is open to talented multicultural students—African American, Asian American, Hispanic American, and Native American.
Housing:	Participants are housed in the college dormitories and have meals in the dining halls.
Costs:	None
Credits Given:	Three college credits for FOCUS 3
Contact:	Stephen MacDonald
	FOCUS Program in Mathematics and Science
	Dickinson College
	Office of Admissions
	Carlisle, PA 17013
	(717) 245-1231; FAX (717) 245-1442

Gallaudet Summer Science Program

Participants have an opportunity to work with other deaf and hard-of-hearing students to solve scientific problems using the facilities, computers, and laboratories of Gallaudet University. Each student is assigned to a research team that conducts experiments in biology, chemistry, or physics under the guidance of professors and instructors. Follow-up activities are continued through the academic year as students use materials provided in take-home science kits with students reporting results. In addition to the academic program, students interact with deaf adults employed as professional scientists and participate in career education workshops. Through "Personal Discovery," an adventure-based program, students are challenged with individual and group problem-solving activities. A recreational program is also provided. *Application deadline: May 1.*

Host School:	Gallaudet University
Type:	Science
Location:	Washington, D.C.
Duration:	Four weeks
Dates:	Late June through late July
Qualifications:	Entering grades 9 through 11. Open to deaf and hard-of-hearing students who want to learn more about science.
Housing:	Participants are housed in the dormitories and have meals in the dining hall.
Costs:	$200
Credits Given:	None
Contact:	Gallaudet Summer Science Program
	Gallaudet University
	HMB 153
	800 Florida Avenue NE
	Washington, DC 20002-3695
	(202) 651-5550; FAX (202) 651-5759

Honors Summer Math Camp: A Young Scholars Program

The Summer Math Camp seeks to stimulate students interested in mathematics by providing them with challenging courses and interesting seminars and activities. Classes address topics not available at the students' home schools. Participants take a class in Elementary Number Theory to provide a solid foundation, and another in Problem Solving to precisely describe and model processes encountered in a wide variety of related word problems. Students utilize Mathematica software in the computer lab to explore the application of ideas discussed in the classroom. An honors seminar is designed to familiarize all students with the opportunities available in the field of mathematics. In other sessions, students engage in discussions about ethical issues in science, career options, and goal setting. Each student is also assigned a faculty mentor who helps the student devise a project to be worked on during the coming school year. Weekly seminars by outstanding professionals, as well as weekend field trips and social and cultural activities, complete this challenging program. Students also have access to the university's athletic and recreational facilities and are automatically admitted to the university's Honors Program. **_Application deadline: April 30._**

Host School:	Southwest Texas State University
Type:	Mathematics
Location:	San Marcos, TX
Duration:	Six weeks
Dates:	Mid-June through late July
Qualifications:	Entering grades 10 through 12. Open to outstanding high school students excited about doing mathematics.
Housing:	Participants are housed in a residence hall and have meals in the dining hall.
Costs:	$100 activity fee. All program expenses including room and board, tuition, and books, as well as a $10 weekly stipend for personal spending money is provided. Additional money for travel expenses is available on an as-needed basis.
Credits Given:	None
Contact:	Dr. Max Warshauer
	Honors Summer Math Camp
	Southwest Texas State University
	601 University Drive
	San Marcos, TX 78666-4616
	(512) 245-3439; FAX (512) 245-3847

Howard Hughes Trainee Program

This program seeks a solution to the problem that some students intensely interested in the biological sciences may not have developed the mathematical skills needed for success in scientific study. Students selected for the program are given the opportunity to improve their mathematical abilities through intensive skills classes and tutoring sessions. Participants are taught to tutor others and are encouraged to use these skills as paid tutors during the coming school year. In addition to the math skills classes, students spend part of each day working as a member of an ongoing research team in an area of the students' personal interest, chosen from a variety of biological and medical research projects. Selection is competitive; at least half the positions are given to women and/or minorities. ***Application deadline: February 19.***

Host School:	University of Nevada, Reno
Type:	Mathematics Study and Biological Sciences Internship
Location:	Reno, NV
Duration:	Seven weeks
Dates:	Mid-June through end of July
Qualifications:	Entering grade 12 and first year of college. Designed for students with a strong interest in the biological sciences, but who may have experienced difficulty in mathematics courses. Applicants must be United States citizens or permanent residents. Women, minorities, and physically disabled students are especially encouraged to apply.
Housing:	Housing is provided for students who will be entering the University of Nevada, Reno, in the fall term. High-school-age trainees may attend as commuters.
Costs:	Students selected for this program receive a stipend of $2,000 for the seven-week period.
Credits Given:	One college credit in biology, chemistry, or biochemistry
Contact:	Dr. Alan Gubanich
	Howard Hughes Trainee Program
	University of Nevada, Reno
	College of Arts and Sciences - 086
	Reno, NV 89557
	(702) 784-6155; FAX (702) 784-1478

Institute for Pre-college Enrichment: MITE Minority Introduction to Engineering

This workshop seeks to stimulate the interest of the participants in careers in engineering and architecture. Emphasis is on mathematics, problem solving, and visualization. Students are taught to approach problems from an engineering point of view. Career awareness activities and opportunities for interaction with professionals working in these fields are major components of the program. Selection for the program is competitive; acceptances are made on a rolling basis. *Application deadline: April 1.*

Host School:	Prairie View A & M University
Type:	Engineering and Architecture
Location:	Prairie View, TX
Duration:	Two weeks
Dates:	Two sessions held: middle through late June and middle through late July.
Qualifications:	Entering grades 11 and 12. Open to minority students who rank in the top third of their class and those who are interested in careers in engineering or architecture. United States citizens only are eligible for this program.
Housing:	Participants are housed in the dormitories and have meals in the dining hall.
Costs:	$50 registration and activity fee.
Credits Given:	None
Contact:	Institute for Pre-college Enrichment
	Prairie View A & M University
	P.O. Box 66
	Prairie View, TX 77446-0066
	1 (800) 622-9643 or (409) 857-2055

Institute for Pre-college Enrichment:
SCOPE Science Careers Opportunity Enhancement

Workshops at the Institute are designed to stimulate students' interest in science and technical careers while they experience a taste of college life and get a look at the opportunities available to them at Prairie View A & M. Student participants in SCOPE learn about careers in the health sciences, including the fields of medicine, dentistry, and veterinary medicine. In addition, courses designed to strengthen the basic skills needed by those pursuing health science careers are given. Participants have many chances to interact with professionals working in these fields and to learn about opportunities for future careers. Selection is competitive and on a rolling basis. *Application deadline: April 1.*

Host School:	Prairie View A & M University
Type:	Summer Study
Location:	Prairie View, TX
Duration:	Two weeks
Dates:	Two sessions held: middle through late June and middle through late July.
Qualifications:	Entering grades 10 through 12. Open to serious students who rank in the upper third of their class, who are interested in a career in the health sciences. Students must be United States citizens.
Housing:	Participants are housed in the dormitories and have meals in the dining hall.
Costs:	$50 activity fee.
Credits Given:	None
Contact:	Hal Walker
	Institute for Pre-college Enrichment: SCOPE
	Prairie View A & M University
	P.O. Box 66
	Prairie View, TX 77446-0066
	1 (800) 622-9643 or (409) 857-2055

Jackling Mineral Industries Summer Careers Institute and Jackling-2: A Young Scholars Program

Conducted by the School of Mines and Metallurgy, the Jackling Institute is designed to introduce high school students to career opportunities in ceramic, mining, geological, metallurgical, nuclear, and petroleum engineering and in geology and geophysics. Students participate in lab experiments from each of the seven departments and attend demonstrations and discussions with faculty and students. Twenty student participants from the Institute are invited to participate in August in a three-week National Science Foundation internship during which they work on a research project with a University of Missouri–Rolla faculty member. They also take classes that consider such topics as engineering ethics, the role of science and engineering in society, and challenges to American technology. An oral and written project presentation culminates the summer research experience. A program competition awards $500 to the best research report, with additional cash awards given to second- through fourth-place reports. All Jackling-2 participants are encouraged to enter their projects in other science and engineering competitions. ***Application deadline: April 8.***

Host School:	University of Missouri–Rolla
Type:	Engineering and Geology
Location:	Rolla, MO
Duration:	One week for the Summer Career Institute program; four weeks for Jackling-2
Dates:	Three sessions: early, mid-, and late June for introductory program. Jackling-2 takes place in August.
Qualifications:	Entering grade 12. Open to students interested in the environmental, energy, materials, or minerals disciplines. Jackling-2 candidates are selected from introductory participants.
Housing:	Participants are housed in the dormitories and have meals in the dining hall.
Costs:	$85 for introductory program. No student cost for Jackling-2. Students selected for the August research experience receive a stipend of $255, plus room and board.
Credits Given:	None
Contact:	Dr. Ronald Kohser
	Jackling Mineral Industries Summer Careers Institute
	University of Missouri–Rolla
	School of Mines and Metallurgy
	305 McNutt Hall
	Rolla, MO 65401
	(314) 341-4734; FAX (314) 341-4192

Maryland Summer Center:
Western Maryland Science Center Program

"All parts of the ecosystem are interrelated." Students in this interesting summer program explore these relationships through activities that include netting a trout in a mountain stream, exploring an old-growth forest, and hiking in the mountains. Experts in the areas of forestry, wildlife, water, and soil conduct field investigations with students to help them learn firsthand about the habitats that exist within the ecosystem. Students gain a working knowledge of the functioning of a mountain ecosystem through chemical water tests, fish surveys, studies of forestry practices, and soil testing. Almost all program time is spent in the field. Evening trips to an area historical museum and to a modern pulp and paper mill allow students to compare old and new techniques. Recreational activities include a canoe trip down the Potomac River, followed by a picnic and bluegrass music. *Application deadline: Early April.*

Host School:	Frostburg State Univesity
Type:	Environmental Science
Location:	Frostburg, MD
Duration:	One week
Dates:	Mid-July
Qualifications:	Entering grade 6 through 9. Open to students interested in the outdoors and the environment.
Housing:	Participants are housed in dormitories and have meals in the dining hall.
Costs:	$200 for Maryland residents who qualify through the state's gifted and talented program. Out-of-state students pay actual costs (approximately $600). Need-based financial aid is available.
Credits Given:	None
Contact:	John Festerman
	Maryland Summer Center
	Board of Education of Allegany County
	108 Washington Street, P.O. Box 1724
	Cumberland, MD 21502
	(301) 759-2014

Math and Science for Minority Students (MS²)

This unique program allows selected minority students to begin an intense study of math and science for three consecutive summers. Located on the campus of Phillips Academy, Andover, the oldest incorporated boarding school in the nation, the program offers students challenges to better prepare themselves for possible careers in science and related fields. Nine hours of science and math classes and four hours of English classes (incorporating writing, library skills, and computer literacy) and college counseling sessions occur weekly. Over three summers, participants take biology, chemistry with lab, a physics course, and math courses. MS² students also take part in a full range of athletic and recreational activities and field trips. Senior students visit area colleges each Wednesday. *Application deadline: January 8.*

Host School:	Phillips Academy
Type:	Mathematics and Science
Location:	Andover, MA
Duration:	Six weeks per summer for three summers
Dates:	Beginning of July through mid-August
Qualifications:	Entering grade 10 (for initial program). Open to math- and science-oriented African American and Hispanic students from Atlanta, Baltimore, Boston, Chicago, Cleveland, Dayton, Ft. Worth, Louisville, Memphis, New York, and Washington, D.C., and to any Native American.
Housing:	Participants are housed in the dormitories and have meals in the dining hall.
Costs:	None. Financial aid to meet incidental expenses is available.
Credits Given:	None
Contact:	Mr. Walter Sherrill
	Math and Science for Minority Students
	Phillips Academy
	Director, Math and Science for Minority Students
	Andover, MA 01810
	(508) 749-4402

Mathematical Modeling: Solutions to Real-World Problems

As part of the AEGIS (Academic Enrichment for the Gifted in Summer), the Mathematical Modeling program challenges its participants to use mathematics to solve today's real-world problems. Students consider topics that include inventory control, process scheduling, and decision analysis. Students are taught to use the powerful tools and techniques of mathematical modeling to creatively solve problems. Computers are used extensively to allow students to concentrate on the problem-solving process. The program culminates in a team competition in which students attempt to solve some of the real-world problems addressed by professional consultants. ***Contact the program coordinator for application information.***

Host School:	Harding University
Type:	Mathematics
Location:	Searcy, AR
Duration:	Two weeks
Dates:	Mid-July
Qualifications:	Entering grades 9 through 11. Open to Arkansas students gifted in mathematics who have completed at least one year of algebra.
Housing:	Participants are housed in a residence hall and have meals in the dining facilities.
Costs:	None
Credits Given:	None
Contact:	Steven Smith
	Mathematical Modeling
	Harding University
	Box 764
	Searcy, AR 72149-0001
	(501) 279-4704

Meadowcreek Weeks

Junior high school students interested in environmental science explore various technologies and take part in practical solutions to environmental problems. Meadowcreek Weeks provides seminars, discussion groups, hands-on activities, and experimentation in the fields of agriculture, energy, ecology, and waste management. Students utilize Meadowcreek's 1500-acre outdoor classroom and a field trip to Blancard Springs Caverns to examine the fragile balance of living ecosystems. Work at Meadowcreek's solar-powered education center helps students understand the impact of their own lifestyles on our environment. Meadowcreek Weeks is part of the AEGIS (Academic Enrichment for the Gifted in Summer) program presented by the state of Arkansas. Funding is provided by a grant from the Arkansas Department of Education. *Contact the program coordinator for application deadline.*

Host School:	Meadowcreek
Type:	Environmental Science
Location:	Fox, AR
Duration:	Two weeks
Dates:	Summer. Dates vary from year to year.
Qualifications:	Entering grades 7 and 8. Open to Arkansas students interested in environmental issues.
Housing:	Participants are provided with dormitory housing and meals.
Costs:	None
Credits Given:	None
Contact:	Director
	Meadowcreek Weeks
	Meadowcreek
	P.O. Box 100
	Fox, AR 72051
	(501) 363-4500

Michigan Summer Institute for Technology: Role of Technology in Development of Ideas

This Summer Institute program focuses on the impact of technology in six selected areas: art, music, audio communications, video communications, information technology, and manufacturing technology. Students explore an area of their choice through a problem-solving methodology. In manufacturing technologies, students use a mobile lab to learn about the full product development process from conceptualization through end use. Audio communications students learn audio techniques and discover the capabilities and limitations of audio equipment. Students interested in video production learn appropriate skills needed to produce a television program. The art workshop uses computer graphics to model, paint, and texture images. The music workshop provides hands-on experience with equipment and techniques for producing music electronically. Students interested in information technology experience an overview of the field, including work with computer-based training and technology-assisted information retrieval. Peer group meetings, discussions, and recreational activities occupy evening and weekend time. To enroll, see your high school counselor in January. *Application deadline: February 28.*

Host School:	Spring Arbor College
Type:	Technology and the liberal arts
Location:	Spring Arbor, MI
Duration:	One week
Dates:	June-July
Qualifications:	Entering grades 11 and 12. Open to Michigan residents interested in exploring the impact of technology on modern life.
Housing:	Participants are housed in dormitories and have meals in the dining hall.
Costs:	$200. Financial aid is available.
Credits Given:	None
Contact:	Ms. Violet Rohrer
	Michigan Summer Institute for Technology
	Spring Arbor College
	Director of Continuing Studies
	Spring Arbor, MI 49283
	(517) 750-6368; FAX (517) 750-1604

MIDI—From Bach to Bytes

In this unusual program the fields of music and computer technology are combined. Students gain competence in working with the Macintosh computer, MIDI compatible keyboards, and composition software. Participants use the equipment to create their own music for performance and publication. Through visits to other MIDI labs and to recording studios, and through talks with music experts, students gain an understanding of the impact of both music and computers on their lives. The program is offered as part of the AEGIS (Academic Enrichment for the Gifted in Summer) program of the state of Arkansas. *Contact program coordinator for application deadline.*

Host School:	Jonesboro Public Schools
Type:	Music and Computer Technology
Location:	Jonesboro, AR
Duration:	Two weeks
Dates:	Early to mid-July
Qualifications:	Entering grades 11 and 12. Open to Arkansas students interested in music and computer education.
Housing:	Participants are provided with housing and meals by the Jonesboro public school system.
Costs:	None
Credits Given:	None
Contact:	Gary Morris
	MIDI—From Bach to Bytes
	Jonesboro Public Schools
	301 Hurricane Drive
	Jonesboro, AR 72401
	(501) 935-3031

Minorities in Engineering Program

Participants spend an intensive week exploring careers in the related engineering and scientific disciplines. Fields such as biotechnology, space science, bioengineering, and engineering technology are explored along with careers in electrical, civil, mechanical, geological, chemical, and mining engineering. Each session includes a laboratory experience demonstrating the kinds of information each engineering and science area uses. Students explore these careers through laboratory and field exercises and through conversations with professional engineers and scientists who lend insight into their work. Special informational sessions provide knowledge about cooperative education and military opportunities and college and financial aid information. Participants also have time to discover college life and interact with other young people. Social and recreational activities complete this busy week's program. ***Application deadline: Early April.***

Host School:	Michigan Technological University
Type:	Engineering and Technology
Location:	Houghton, MI
Duration:	One week
Dates:	Mid to late June
Qualifications:	Entering grades 10 through 12. Open to minority and economically disadvantaged students who have a strong mathematics and science background and/or interest in technological studies. Two years of high school math and a year of chemistry are recommended.
Housing:	Participants are housed in the residence halls and have meals in the dining facilities.
Costs:	None. Students pay only a small registration fee.
Credits Given:	None
Contact:	Ms. Kerry Hicks
	Minorities in Engineering Program
	Michigan Technological University
	Youth Programs Office
	1400 Townsend Drive
	Houghton, MI 49931-1295
	(906) 487-2219; FAX (906) 487-3101

Minority Engineering Summer Research Program

This program is designed to give participants a chance to experience college life and the demands of an engineering curriculum while introducing them to a variety of career options available in the field of engineering. Weekday mornings are spent in the classroom; students explore the mathematics and science aspects of engineering and participate in a regular summer school course. Special lectures by industrial leaders and field trips to local industrial sites provide a look at engineering as practiced today. This program is sponsored in part by industrial companies. Afternoons are spent working with a Vanderbilt professor on a research project. *Application deadline: March 1.*

Host School:	Vanderbilt University
Type:	Summer Study/Internship
Location:	Nashville, TN
Duration:	Five weeks
Dates:	Early July through early August
Qualifications:	Entering grade 12 or entering first year of college at Vanderbilt in the fall. Open to minority students. Most of the spaces are for students who will be enrolling at Vanderbilt in the fall, but some spaces are available for qualified high school juniors.
Housing:	Participants are housed in the dormitories and have meals in the dining hall.
Costs:	None. Because students are unable to work for this five-week period, a stipend is provided for each selected student.
Credits Given:	College credits are available.
Contact:	Dr. Carolyn Williams
	Minority Engineering Summer Research Program
	Vanderbilt University
	Vanderbilt University School of Engineering, Office of the Dean
	Box 6006, Station B
	Nashville, TN 37235
	(615) 322-2724

Minority Enrichment Seminar in Engineering Training (MESET)

The Minority Enrichment Seminar in Engineering Training (MESET) program is intended to give gifted minority students the opportunity to become familiar with opportunities in the field of engineering while experiencing life in a university environment. A variety of short courses explore areas of study that include computers, chemistry, math, physics, problem solving, and engineering design. Field trips to industrial facilities on the Gulf Coast, as well as tours of the college facilities, give participants a firsthand look at the work done by practicing engineers. Guest lectures, sports, social events, along with weekend and evening programs, round out the experience. ***Application deadline: April 15.***

Host School:	University of Houston
Type:	Engineering
Location:	Houston, TX
Duration:	Three weeks
Dates:	Early to late June
Qualifications:	Entering grade 12. Open to minority students planning to pursue a career in engineering who have shown an aptitude for engineering study.
Housing:	Participants are housed in dormitories and have meals (with the exception of weekend meals) in the dining hall.
Costs:	None. Weekend meals are not provided and are the responsibility of the students.
Credits Given:	None
Contact:	Dr. G. F. Paskusz
	Minority Enrichment Seminar in Engineering Training
	University of Houston
	PROMES
	4800 Calhoun Rd.
	Houston, TX 77204-4790
	(713) 743-4222

Minority High School Student Research Apprenticeship Program

The program is designed to encourage students to consider careers in scientific research in a health-related field. Each participant spends six weeks conducting a research project under the guidance and direction of a faculty scientist. In addition to their involvement in laboratory research, students may enroll in chemistry, zoology, or psychology classes. At the conclusion of the program, each student participates in a summer science symposium sharing with other students the results of his or her research experience. *Application deadline: April 30.*

Host School: Tennessee State University

Type: Health Science Internship

Location: Nashville, TN

Duration: Six weeks

Dates: Late June through the end of July

Qualifications: Entering grade 12 and first year of college. Open to high-ability minority students—those identifying themselves as Black, Hispanic, American Indian, Alaskan Native, or Pacific Islander/Asian. Applicants must be in the top third of their high school class with an average of B+ or better.

Housing: Participants are housed in dormitories and have meals in the campus dining facilities.

Costs: None

Credits Given: Credits are available for students who choose to take a college class.

Contact: Dr. Robert Newkirk
Minority High School Student Research Apprenticeship Program
Tennessee State University
3500 John A. Merritt Boulevard
Nashville, TN 37209-1561
(615) 320-3462

Minority Introduction to Engineering (MITE): Georgia Tech

The MITE program seeks to encourage minority students to pursue careers in science, technology, and engineering. The program includes presentations in the various scientific and engineering disciplines along with career information and guidance. Students take part in engineering experiments, go on field trips to area industries, and tour the engineering facilities at Georgia Tech. They also are encouraged to interact with engineering students and industry representatives. *Application deadline: March 15.*

Host School:	Georgia Institute of Technology
Type:	Engineering
Location:	Atlanta, GA
Duration:	One week
Dates:	Two sessions beginning in mid-July.
Qualifications:	Entering grade 12. Open to Black, Hispanic, and American Indian students. Students must have minimum scores of 50 verbal and 55 math on the PSAT, or 500 verbal and 550 math on the SAT.
Housing:	Participants are housed in the dormitories and have meals in the dining halls.
Costs:	$100. Scholarships are not available.
Credits Given:	None
Contact:	Minority Introduction to Engineering
	Georgia Institute of Technology
	College of Engineering
	Atlanta, GA 30332-0361
	(404) 894-3354

Minority Introduction to Engineering (MITE): Illinois

The MITE program at Illinois is designed to give the participants a clear picture of engineering as a profession while exposing students to college-level work. The program includes lectures on engineering, small-group experiments, and round-table discussions with students, faculty and professional engineers. Students receive about ten hours of computer-aided-design lab training and college and career counseling. In addition, student teams are assigned projects related to ongoing research and work with a graduate student adviser. Social activities include a range of intramural sports and a dance. ***Application deadline: May 1.***

Host School:	University of Illinois, Urbana-Champaign
Type:	Engineering
Location:	Champaign, IL
Duration:	Two weeks
Dates:	Middle through late July
Qualifications:	Entering grade 12. Open to minority students (African American, Hispanic, and American Indian) with a definite interest in engineering and applied science and who have demonstrated the ability needed to pursue a college education.
Housing:	Participants are housed and have meals in a university-approved residence hall.
Costs:	$25
Credits Given:	None
Contact:	David Powell
	Minority Introduction to Engineering
	University of Illinois, Urbana-Champaign
	College of Engineering
	1308 West Green Street, Room 207
	Urbana, IL 61801-2982
	(217) 244-4974 , (800) 843-5410

Minority Introduction to Engineering (MITE): Tuskegee

MITE is a rigorous summer program that seeks to introduce minority students to the field of engineering through an in-depth exposure to the various engineering disciplines. In the classroom, students develop skills needed for success in college classes; work focuses on chemistry, mathematics, physics, and engineering theory. Laboratory experiments provide hands-on learning. Presentations by both engineering faculty and practicing engineers, and field trips to industrial and laboratory facilities, provide students with a close look at careers in engineering. During this week, students are totally immersed in campus life and have access to campus facilities, including the libraries, athletic complex, and health services. **Application deadline: April 30.**

Host School:	Tuskegee University
Type:	Engineering
Location:	Tuskegee Institute, AL
Duration:	One week
Dates:	Mid-June
Qualifications:	Entering grade 12. Open to minority students considering careers in engineering.
Housing:	Participants are housed in dormitories and have meals in the dining hall.
Costs:	None
Credits Given:	None
Contact:	Dr. Shaik Jeelani
	Minority Introduction to Engineering
	Tuskegee University
	Associate Dean
	School of Engineering and Architecture
	Tuskegee Institute, AL 36088
	(205) 727-8946

Minority Introduction to Engineering (MITE): United States Coast Guard Academy

The MITE program at the United States Coast Guard Academy is designed to familiarize high school students with the various fields of engineering and to give them a taste of life at the Coast Guard Academy. Participants attend daily sessions centered around the engineering disciplines and learn about career opportunities in engineering through laboratory work and field trips. A special feature of this MITE program allows the participants to experience aspects of military training if they wish to. Evenings are devoted to involvement in athletic activities, tours of the Coast Guard Academy, and interaction between participants and cadets. *Application deadline: March 15.*

Host School:	United States Coast Guard Academy
Type:	Enginering
Location:	New London, CT
Duration:	One week
Dates:	Mid-July
Qualifications:	Entering grade 11. Open to minority students who have an interest in an engineering career and who have an A or B average in school. Scores of at least 95 on the PSAT, 950 on the SAT, or 40 (combined English and math) on the ACT are required.
Housing:	Participants are housed in dormitories and have meals in the dining facilities.
Costs:	None
Credits Given:	None
Contact:	Lieutenant (jg) Catherine Tobias, USCG
	Minority Introduction to Engineering
	c/o Director of Admissions
	15 Mohegan Avenue
	New London, CT 06320
	(203) 447-2897

Minority Introduction to Engineering Program (MITE): Virginia

MITE seeks to introduce interested minority students to the fields of engineering and science, and to acquaint them with the academic demands of an undergraduate engineering curriculum. The program includes daily mathematics classes, followed by lectures, demonstrations, experiments and field trips, introducing participants to specific engineering disciplines. Special attention is given to the fields of aerospace; chemical, civil, electrical, mechanical, systems, and nuclear engineering; and to applied mathematics, engineering science, and computer science. Interaction with University of Virginia professors provides answers to questions about engineering careers and addresses the special concerns of minority students. ***Application deadline: May 7.***

Host School:	University of Virginia
Type:	Engineering
Location:	Charlottesville, VA
Duration:	One week
Dates:	Late July
Qualifications:	Entering grades 11 and 12. Open to minority students (African Americans, Puerto Ricans, Mexican Americans, and Native Americans) who have demonstrated exceptional performance in math and science classes, have a minimum of a B average, and an interest in science and engineering.
Housing:	Participants are housed in dormitories and have meals in the dining facilities.
Costs:	$150. Some need-based scholarships are available.
Credits Given:	None
Contact:	Ron Price
	Minority Introduction to Engineering Program
	University of Virginia
	School of Engineering and Applied Science
	A 127 Thornton Hall
	Charlottesville, VA 22901
	(804) 924-3518

Minority Scholars in Computer Science and Engineering

This six-week program is an exploration of the educational and career opportunities to be found in the fields of computer science and engineering. The academic experience is provided through two college-level courses. In An Introduction to the Engineering Design Process, students work in teams to design and build a product. The second course, Pascal Programming, is an introduction to computer programming using structured programming concepts. Students learn to design and analyze programs written in Pascal. Field trips to the United States Army Research Laboratory, Aberdeen Proving Ground, as well as to other sites in the Washington/Baltimore region, supplement the academic experience. Participating students live in the residence halls at Howard University, and take classes both at the University of Maryland and Howard.
Application deadline: May 10.

Host School:	University of Maryland and Howard University
Type:	Computer Science and Engineering
Location:	College Park, MD
Duration:	Six weeks
Dates:	Late June through early August
Qualifications:	Entering grade 12. Open to African American, Hispanic, and Native American students. Selection is based on academic ability, GPA, PSAT or SAT scores (minimum 1000 combined, 550 Math) and recommendations.
Housing:	Participants are housed in the dormitories and have meals in the dining hall.
Costs:	None for tuition, fees, and housing. Students are responsible for the cost of their own meals.
Credits Given:	Six college credits
Contact:	Ms. Rosemary Parker
	Minority Scholars in Computer Science and Engineering
	University of Maryland
	Center for Minorities in Science and Engineering
	College Park, MD 20742
	(301) 405-3878

Mission Mars

Students interested in space exploration get a chance to consider the problems that confront scientists and discover the answers through their classes at Mission Mars. Participants seek answers to questions that include: How can a permanent manned presence be established on one of the planets? What life support systems would be required? What psychological factors are important in extended space flights or during long periods of isolation? What would be learned by a visit to Mars? Students also have an opportunity to observe current research efforts between Harding University and NASA. Mission Mars is part of the AEGIS (Academic Enrichment for the Gifted in Summer) program. *Application deadline: Contact the program coodinator.*

Host School:	Harding University
Type:	Space science
Location:	Searcy, AR
Duration:	Two weeks
Dates:	Middle through late June
Qualifications:	Entering grades 8 and 9. Open to Arkansas students interested in space and space exploration.
Housing:	Participants are housed in the dormitories and have meals in the dining halls.
Costs:	None
Credits Given:	None
Contact:	Steve Baber
	Mission Mars
	Harding University
	Box 763
	Searcy, AR 72149-0001
	(501) 279-4266

MIT MITES—Minority Introduction to Engineering & Science

This rigorous program introduces minority high school students to careers in science and engineering. Classroom work centers on math, physics, biology and chemistry, humanities, and writing and design. Daily assignments are given. Both individual and group tutoring sessions are held most evenings. Highlighting the program are design contests aimed at developing student solutions to specified problems. Career exploration is provided through presentations by faculty and practicing engineers and scientists. Also included are field trips to area installations and industries. Social events such as a harbor cruise and dance fill weekends and holidays; students also enjoy a trip to a major league baseball game. *Application deadline: February 18.*

Host School: Massachusetts Institute of Technology
Type: Science and Engineering
Location: Cambridge, MA
Duration: Six weeks
Dates: Late June through early August
Qualifications: Entering grade 12. Open to minority students (American Indian, Black American, Mexican American, and Puerto Rican) who have demonstrated above-average ability and have an interest in the study of science and mathematics. Applicants should have completed precalculus or trigonometry.
Housing: Participants are housed in dormitories and have meals in the dining halls.
Costs: None. A limited amount of financial aid is available to help needy students with transportation costs.
Credits Given: None
Contact: MIT MITES—Minority Introduction to Engineering & Science
Massachusetts Institute of Technology
77 Massachusetts Avenue, Room 1-211
Cambridge, MA 02139
(617) 253-8051

MITE: Minority Introduction to Engineering

Designed to give minority students a chance to sample careers in engineering, the Purdue MITE program offers two weeks of career exploration activities. Laboratory sessions, computer work, and tours explore engineering fields including robotics, electron microscopy, computer-assisted drafting, aeronautical engineering, and civil and biomedical engineering. Lectures by faculty members and professional engineers address topics that include Engineering as a Career, Preparing for College, and Financial Aid and Cooperative Education. Through discussions with student and practicing engineers, participants get a clear idea of how engineering training can be used to meet the challenges of the future. Recreational and sports activities are also available. ***Application deadline: May 28.***

Host School:	Purdue University
Type:	Engineering
Location:	West Lafayette, IN
Duration:	Two weeks
Dates:	Mid-July
Qualifications:	Entering grade 12. Open to minority students (African American, American Indian, Mexican American, and Puerto Rican) who have demonstrated an interest in mathematics, engineering, or science.
Housing:	Participants are housed in a residence hall and have meals in the dining facility.
Costs:	$150.
Credits Given:	None
Contact:	MITE: Minority Introduction to Engineering
	Purdue University
	Enad Room 214
	West Lafayette, IN 47907-1286
	(317) 494-3974; FAX (317) 494-5819

Modeling Acid Deposition: An Introduction to Scientific Methods, NSF Young Scholars Program

Students are introduced to scientific methodology through a project studying acid rain deposition. The program includes lecture, laboratory, and field trip activities. Classroom lectures address relevant topics in biology, chemistry, and statistics. Laboratory work in biology and chemistry is combined with extensive computer work. Using statistical methods, small groups of participants study acid rain data, developing predictive models. Field trips take participants to a coal-burning plant, to the Midwest Energy coal facility, and on a three-day camping trip to Vilas County to enjoy the beauty of northern Wisconsin. Recreational trips include a canoe trip, picnics, park visits, and a trip on a Lake Superior research vessel. Evening and weekend social and educational events are planned. **Application deadline: April 17.**

Host School:	University of Wisconsin, Superior
Type:	Biology, Chemistry, Computers, and Mathematics
Location:	Superior, WI
Duration:	Five weeks
Dates:	Late June through late July
Qualifications:	Entering grades 11 and 12. Open to high-ability and high-potential students interested in science and mathematics. Students must have completed classes in geometry, intermediate algebra, chemistry, and biology.
Housing:	Participants are housed in the dormitory and have weekday meals in the cafeteria. Participants provide their own weekend meals.
Costs:	None. Participants are responsible for the cost of most weekend meals. Students who successfully complete the program receive a $100 stipend. Additional aid and transportation costs are available to students with financial need.
Credits Given:	None
Contact:	Dr. Francis Florey
	Modeling Acid Deposition
	University of Wisconsin, Superior
	Mathematics Department
	1800 Grand Avenue
	Superior, WI 54880
	(715) 394-8322; FAX (715) 394-8454

Modern Computer Applications: Michigan Summer Institute

Computers now affect every aspect of modern life. Students can utilize this workshop to apply state-of-the-art techniques to a broad range of computer uses. Participants study computer-related topics including robotics and automation, computer-aided drafting and design (CAD), programmable logic controllers, computer simulation in automotive design, computer-aided manufacturing (CAM), and radiotelemetry. Students generate a CAD drawing for a product of their choice and then manufacture it using CAM. Exercises and discussions about technological issues and concepts in engineering and environmental sciences provide students with both knowledge and confidence to solve problems. Students obtain a real-world view of computer applications on visits to the Soo Locks and Mackinac Bridge. The chief engineers of these facilities are available for student discussion. An optional trip to Canada provides students with supervised, expert instruction in rappelling. Social and recreational activities complete the program. For further information contact David McDonald at (906) 635-2207, or write to contact listed below. **Application deadline: February 28.**

Host School:	Lake Superior State University
Type:	Computer Science
Location:	Sault Sainte Marie, MI
Duration:	One week
Dates:	Mid-July
Qualifications:	Entering grades 11 and 12. Open to Michigan residents interested in exploring computer applications in mechanical, electrical, and environmental engineering and robotics. Strong mathematics and basic computer operation skills are encouraged.
Housing:	Participants are housed in the dormitories and take meals in the dining facilities.
Costs:	$200. Financial aid is available.
Credits Given:	None
Contact:	Chris Kitzman
	Modern Computer Applications Program
	Ingham Intermediate School District
	2630 West Howell Road
	Mason, MI 48854
	(517) 676-2550

The National Science Foundation's (NSF) Young Scholars

The National Science Foundation (NSF) began its Young Scholars Programs in 1988, with the goal of exciting students entering grades 7 through 12 about science. Student participants are encouraged to investigate and possibly pursue careers in science, mathematics, engineering, and technology. Numerous programs funded by NSF are offered each summer, enabling the directors to provide this experience to interested students at little or no cost. Most of the programs feature intensive study in the field of the student's interest, such as mathematics, physics, archaeology, or marine biology. Laboratory exercises and visits to area industries and research laboratories provide extensions to daily lessons. Students gain both a greater understanding of their specific discipline and a real-world view of the applications of their studies to modern life. Since the programs are held on college campuses, field research sites, and scientific laboratories, students have the opportunity to use state-of-the-art equipment and computers, while interacting with professional scientists excited about their work. Students also participate in a full range of sports and recreational activities. *See contact below for further information about program.*

Host School:	Selected colleges and universities across the United States
Type:	Science, Engineering, Mathematics, Computer Science, and Technology Study and Research Programs
Location:	On campuses throughout the United States
Duration:	Two to eight weeks
Dates:	Various dates during the summer months
Qualifications:	Programs are directed to middle school and high school students interested in intensive experiences in science and technology.
Housing:	Most programs provide housing and meals for their participants.
Costs:	Most programs are offered at either very minimal cost or no charge to participants. Some programs provide a stipend to the students.
Credits Given:	Some programs offer high school or college credits.
Contact:	The National Science Foundation's Young Scholars Programs National Science Foundation 4201 Wilson Boulevard, Room 885 Arlington, VA 22230 (703) 306-1616

National Youth Science Camp (NYSC)

National Youth Science Camp (NYSC) provides a truly unique educational forum held in a beautiful rustic camp setting in the eastern highlands of West Virginia. Scientists from across the nation present lectures on the most current topics, including the human genome project, ozone depletion, AIDS, robotics, and the fate of our rain forests. Participants pursue their own research projects in the camp's laboratories and field research stations, engaging in informal discussions with prominent scientists. Free time and weekends find the delegates participating in a wide range of athletic activities, including fishing, rock climbing, kayaking, caving, and backpacking. A highlight of the program is a three-day trip to Washington, D.C., where participants lunch with senators and tour cultural sites and scientific facilities such as the NASA/Goddard Space Flight Center. *Application deadline: Contact program, guidance counselor, or your State Department of Education for information.*

Host School:	National Youth Science Foundation, Inc.
Type:	Science
Location:	Near Bartow, WV
Duration:	Three and a half weeks
Dates:	Late June through late July
Qualifications:	Two graduating seniors from each state are chosen annually, based on academic achievements, leadership abilities, well-rounded interests, and intent to pursue a career in science or mathematics. Selection is competitive.
Housing:	Delegates live at a rustic camp near Bartow in the eastern part of West Virginia's Potomac Highlands. The camp is located within the wilderness areas of the Monongahela National Forest. Meals are taken in the dining facilities.
Costs:	None. All expenses, including transportation, are provided.
Credits Given:	None
Contact:	National Youth Science Camp
	National Youth Science Foundation, Inc.
	P.O. Box 3387
	Charleston, WV 25333
	(304) 342-3326

The New Jersey Governor's School in the Sciences

The Governor's School in the Sciences seeks to broaden its participants' appreciation and knowledge of science, provide career exploration, and introduce students to scientific research. Students select a core of three courses from choices that include biology, chemistry, computer science, mathematics, and physics. Each student selects a lab course that meets twice a week. Evening electives include such topics as lasers, forensic science, space science, and philosophy of science. Two afternoons a week are set aside for team projects in which students work as part of a small research team studying in areas of student interest, such as celestial mechanics, holography, psychology, computer software development, and ecosystems. One day of each week is devoted to field trips to local science labs and sites such as AT&T Bell labs, Exxon Research, the University of Medicine & Dentistry, and Celanese. Evening colloquium speakers and small group seminars allow students to learn about science from both industrial and academic viewpoints. During free time, students have access to Drew University's athletic facilities and take part in group trips to the Shakespeare Festival, films, and sporting events. Special events include a selective college fair and career morning. ***Application deadline: January 4.***

Host School:	Drew University
Type:	Science
Location:	Madison, NJ
Duration:	Four weeks
Dates:	July
Qualifications:	Entering grade 12. Open to talented New Jersey students who want to explore new knowledge and acquire higher-level skills than those currently available to them in high school.
Housing:	Participants are housed in dormitories and have meals in the dining facilities.
Costs:	None
Credits Given:	None
Contact:	Jim Keen
	The New Jersey Governor's School in the Sciences
	Drew University
	Madison, NJ 07940
	(908) 571-3496; FAX (908) 571-7556

$\mathbb{T}$he New Jersey Governor's School on the Environment

This program offers students an intensive learning experience exploring the relationships between human beings and their impact on one another and the environment. The program encourages student development by providing them with both skills and knowledge to become community leaders. Another goal is to increase student sensitivity to our fragile ecosystems. The program is structured around an intensive course focusing on specific areas such as environmental protection, global ecosystems, and the quality of urban life. Small-group seminars further explore issues. Frequent field trips provide experience with multiple habitats, as well as opportunities for research. Evening programs further enrich learning and may include debates, lectures, simulations, and workshops. Students are also encouraged to take part in the program's visual and performing arts component. Professional performing arts events and social activities complete this stimulating program. *Application deadline: January 4.*

Host School:	Stockton State College
Type:	Environmental Science
Location:	Pomona, NJ
Duration:	Four weeks
Dates:	July
Qualifications:	Entering grade 12. Open to gifted New Jersey students interested in exploring environmental challenges, including not only those of the natural environment, but also those of the social, economic, and political environments.
Housing:	Participants are housed in the dormitories and have meals in the dining facilities.
Costs:	None
Credits Given:	None
Contact:	The New Jersey Governor's School on the Environment
	Stockton State College
	Pomona, NJ 08240-9988
	(609) 652-4924

North Dakota Governor's School in Science and Mathematics

The North Dakota Governor's School provides an intensive summer experience in science and mathematics. All students begin their day with an hourlong creative thinking session that focuses discussion on personal and social issues. The students are then divided into mathematical sciences and laboratory sciences study groups for the remainder of the day. Mathematics students study mathematics theory, research methods, data analysis, and computer science. While engaged in computer science, students learn to "surf the Internet" and view the World Wide Web. Students taking part in the laboratory sciences curriculum begin their program by becoming familiar with laboratory equipment and techniques through performance of experiments in a biochemistry teaching laboratory. By the end of the first week, each student chooses a research topic and is placed in a faculty member's laboratory to conduct experiments. Evenings and weekends are utilized for special programs that include fine arts activities (photography, band, art, drama, creative writing) and discussions on ethics. Field trips, recreational and career exploration activities, and volunteer projects occupy some of the participants' nonprogram time. ***Application deadline: February 1.***

Host School:	North Dakota State University
Type:	Science and Mathematics
Location:	Fargo, ND
Duration:	Six weeks
Dates:	Early June through mid-July
Qualifications:	Entering grades 11 and 12. Open to North Dakota students with above-average ability and interest in science and/or mathematics.
Housing:	Participants are housed in the residence halls and have meals in the dining hall.
Costs:	None
Credits Given:	None
Contact:	Dr. Allan Fischer
	North Dakota Governor's School in Science and Mathematics
	North Dakota State University
	College of Science and Mathematics
	Fargo, ND 58105
	(701) 231-7411; FAX (701) 231-7149

Northeast Science Enrichment Program

The Northeast Science Enrichment Program seeks to encourage underrepresented and underserved students to consider careers in science and mathematics by exposing them to these fields at an early age. Hands-on courses in biology, physics, math, chemistry, computer science, and language arts are combined with a variety of other educational experiences. Field trips to the Boston Science Museum, data collection on the research vessel *Envirolab*, and seminars by scientists broaden the participant's background. Daily recreational activities and a variety of cultural events complete the program. ***Application deadline: April 1.***

Host School:	University of Massachusetts at Amherst
Type:	Science and Mathematics
Location:	Amherst, MA
Duration:	Five weeks
Dates:	Mid-July through mid-August
Qualifications:	Entering grade 10. Open to motivated minority (African Americans, Hispanic Americans, Native Americans) and underserved (poor, rural, disadvantaged) students from Connecticut, New Hampshire, Maine, Massachusetts, upper New York, Rhode Island, and Vermont.
Housing:	Participants are housed in the dormitories and have meals in the dining facilities.
Costs:	None.
Credits Given:	None
Contact:	Northeast Science Enrichment Program
	University of Massachusetts at Amherst
	Department of Mathematics and Statistics
	Lederle Graduate Research Center
	Amherst, MA 01003
	(413) 545-1909; FAX (413) 545-1801

Nurse Camp

Nurse camp is a residential program designed to provide participants with an educational experience about the nursing profession. Students visit a number of area sites to experience nursing as it is practiced in settings that include hospitals, nursing homes, clinics, home health agencies, hospices, and community hospitals. Students learn nursing skills such as basic first aid, cardiopulmonary resuscitation, glucose monitoring, blood pressure reading, and patient/caregiver interactions. A career and college counseling component provides students with advice on the high school course work that will best prepare students for health care careers, as well as information on financing a nursing education. *Application deadline: March 21.*

Host School:	University of Wisconsin, Madison
Type:	Nursing careers
Location:	Madison, WI
Duration:	One week
Dates:	Mid-June
Qualifications:	Open to high school students ages 13 through 18 who are interested in careers in nursing.
Housing:	Participants are housed in dormitories and have meals in the dining halls.
Costs:	None
Credits Given:	None
Contact:	Nurse Camp
	University of Wisconsin, Madison
	600 Highland Avenue
	Madison, WI 53792
	(608) 263-5183; FAX (608) 263-5332

Nursing Precollege Program for Minority Middle School Students

Nurses are in demand all across the country as the need for quality health care has increased. The Nursing Precollege Program provides middle school students with an opportunity for firsthand exploration of nursing as a career. Students visit hospitals, primary health care sites, and other health care delivery facilities to see the range of settings in which nurses are employed. Hands-on experiences in a nursing skills laboratory find students taking pulses and blood pressure. Academic sessions concentrate on necessary study skills, mathematics, and writing. Participants are also paired with nurse mentors and observe them in practice. Students who complete this exciting week will have a clear view of the field of nursing as a possible future career and an understanding of the educational path to be followed to become a professional nurse. *Application deadline: March 15.*

Host School:	University of Wisconsin, Madison
Type:	Nursing Careers
Location:	Madison, WI
Duration:	One week
Dates:	Late June
Qualifications:	Students entering grades 7 through 9. Open to minority and disadvantaged students who reside in the Madison, Janesville, and Beloit areas.
Housing:	Participants are housed in a residence hall and have meals in the dining facilities.
Costs:	$25. A number of need-based scholarships are available.
Credits Given:	None
Contact:	Nursing Precollege Program
	University of Wisconsin, Madison
	School of Nursing
	600 Highland Avenue
	Madison, WI 53792-2455
	(608) 262-5606 or 263-5183; FAX (608) 263-5332

Ohio Governor's Institute for Gifted and Talented Students

Students desiring a real taste of college life and learning will find Wittenberg's program of interest. Students may choose to attend either or both sessions. One session, entitled "Probing Mind and Behavior," explores the science of psychology. Through intensive hands-on experiments, students study brain physiology, sensation, learning, and abnormal behavior and therapy, all of which lead to an understanding of animal and human behavior. Field activities, demonstrations, and group problem solving round out this program that introduces a full range of activity from lab research to therapeutic application. Natural science students might choose the session titled "Living Waters: A Molecular Understanding of Aquatic Ecosystems." This session allows students to experience the scientific process through field testing, lab verification, and mathematical analysis. Participants analyze samples collected during a field trip, studying such factors as populations, gas concentrations, nutrients, and toxic substances. The microcomputer lab is used to perform computer simulations and statistical analyses. Students in both sessions use the university facilities, including science and computer labs, library, and athletic complex. Evening activities complement the program. *Application deadline: April 11.*

Host School:	Wittenberg University
Type:	Psychology and Ecology Workshops
Location:	Springfield, OH
Duration:	One week
Dates:	Two sessions are held from early through mid-July.
Qualifications:	Entering grades 10 and 11. Open to Ohio residents interested in psychology and/or ecology.
Housing:	Participants are housed in a dormitory and have meals in the student dining room.
Costs:	$172 for room and meals.
Credits Given:	None
Contact:	Dr. Barbara Mackey
	Ohio Governor's Institute for Gifted and Talented Students
	Wittenberg University
	P.O. Box 720
	Spingfield, OH 45501-0720
	(513) 327-7050; FAX (513) 327-6340

Ohio Governor's Summer Institute: Engineering Careers

Students interested in possible future careers in engineering will find this program provides an overview of many of the engineering disciplines. Students take part in hands-on experiences that provide a look at aerospace, electrical, mechanical, chemical, civil, and optics engineering. Participants explore such topics as the aerodynamics of airplane wings, applications of computers in electrical engineering, electrical circuit designs, mechanical and chemical engineering experiments, CAD/CAM/CAE computer-assisted design, design of digital computers, and column design in civil engineering. Through interaction with the Air Force Institute of Technology researchers and a field trip to Wright-Patterson Air Force Base, students are provided with a close look at real-world engineering applications and careers. *Application deadline: April 11.*

Host School: The University of Dayton

Type: Engineering

Location: Dayton, OH

Duration: One week

Dates: Three sessions are held from late June through mid-July.

Qualifications: Entering grades 10 and 11. Open to motivated Ohio students interested in exploring options for careers in engineering.

Housing: Participants are housed in the dormitories and have meals in the dining halls.

Costs: $100 per session for room and board.

Credits Given: None

Contact: Dr. Thomas Matczynski
Ohio Governor's Summer Institute
The University of Dayton
318 Chaminade Hall
Dayton, OH 45469-0534
(513) 229-3734

Pennsylvania Governor's School for the Agricultural Sciences (PGSAS)

Because agricultural research and policy are so important to today's global economy, the Pennsylvania Department of Education, along with Penn State University, offers high-ability students the opportunity to explore the world of agricultural science. Participants attend classes in agricultural science and technology. With faculty members, students engage in an independent study project in their choice of such areas as nutrition, animal biochemistry, wildlife management, land use planning, and computer monitoring systems. A special feature of the Governor's School is a leadership component in which students learn how to share their special skills and knowledge with others. Seminars on current issues, field trips to agricultural agencies and industries, hands-on sessions in labs, greenhouses, and farms, along with college and career counseling, complete the program. Students also participate in social and recreational activities. Graduates of this program are eligible for special scholarships at Pennsylvania universities. *Application deadline: Early February.*

Host School:	Penn State University
Type:	Agricultural and Environmental Science
Location:	University Park, PA
Duration:	Five weeks
Dates:	Early July through early August
Qualifications:	Entering grades 11 and 12. Open to Pennsylvania students with a demonstrated ability in science, food, agriculture, or natural resources. Former Governor's School participants are ineligible.
Housing:	Participants are housed and have meals in the residence halls.
Costs:	None
Credits Given:	None
Contact:	Dr. Marianne Houser
	Pennsylvania Governor's School for the Agricultural Sciences
	Penn State University
	101 Agricultural Administration Building
	University Park, PA 16802
	(814) 865-7521 or (717) 524-5244; FAX (814) 863-7277

Pennsylvania Governor's School for the Health Care Professions

Funded and developed by the Hospital Association of Pennsylvania in cooperation with the Governor's Schools, the program provides participants with classes, observational experiences, independent research, and the opportunity to shadow health care professionals as they work. The program enrolls students interested in medicine, dentistry, nursing, physical therapy, pharmacy, and occupational therapy, among other health care professions. Students take a curriculum composed of core courses that explore topics such as the body systems, the influence of health and illness on the family, financing health care, and the impact of biotechnology on the quality of life. Throughout the program, students take part in hands-on exercises, discussions, and lectures that stress the importance of team work in health care delivery. Specialty courses on topics that include chronic disease, sports and rehabilitative medicine, environmental and public health, and mental health place students in learning teams that ultimately present a program to the entire group. Recreation and field trips complete this exciting program. *Application deadline: Early February.*

Host School:	University of Pittsburgh
Type:	Health Sciences
Location:	Pittsburgh, PA
Duration:	Five weeks
Dates:	Early July through early August
Qualifications:	Entering grade 12. Open to Pennsylvania students interested in pursuing careers in health care and human service. Former Governor's School participants are ineligible.
Housing:	Participants are housed in the dormitories and have meals in the dining facilities.
Costs:	None
Credits Given:	None
Contact:	Pennsylvania Governor's School for the Health Care Professions University of Pittsburgh Pittsburgh, PA Information Hotline: (717) 524-5244

Pennsylvania Governor's School for the Sciences

This program provides outstanding students with an advanced curriculum and unique research experiences. Students take core courses including molecular biology, chemistry, physics, discrete mathematics, and computer science. Additional elective classes in astrophysics, biochemistry, nuclear chemistry, mathematics, and the philosophy of science are also offered. Students select one laboratory course from a number offered and work as a member of a collaborative research team on a project of their choice. Students present their project at a student exhibition at the conclusion of the summer. The program also includes workshops in which students learn about group dynamics and practice leadership techniques. Educational guidance sessions, interaction with guest scientists, and field trips and tours of area facilities round out the learning experience. Recreational and social activities occur during evenings and weekends. Graduates of the program become eligible for special scholarships at Pennsylvania universities. *Application deadline: January 19.*

Host School:	Carnegie Mellon University
Type:	Science, Mathematics, and Computer Science
Location:	Pittsburgh, PA
Duration:	Five weeks
Dates:	End of June through early August
Qualifications:	Entering grade 12. Open to Pennsylvania students with outstanding ability in science and math. Former Governor's School participants are ineligible.
Housing:	Participants are housed in the dormitories and have their meals in the dining facilities.
Costs:	No program costs.
Credits Given:	None
Contact:	Pennsylvania Governor's School for the Sciences
	Carnegie Mellon University
	Doherty Hall 2201
	Schenley Park
	Pittsburgh, PA 15213
	Information hotline: (717) 524-5244 or (412) 268-6669

Pre-engineering Summer Workshops for Women and Minorities

The Pre-engineering Summer Workshops are designed to introduce students to the field of engineering. Students have an opportunity to explore the various engineering disciplines through experiments, problem solving, tours of laboratories and engineering facilities, and presentations by practicing engineers. A number of commuter programs are also offered for women and minority students who have completed grades 8 through 12. Contact program director for more information. *Application deadline: March 31.*

Host School:	University of Arizona
Type:	Engineering
Location:	Tucson, AZ
Duration:	Three to eight days
Dates:	Four sessions are held during June
Qualifications:	Entering grades 8 through 12. Competitive admissions for female and minority students interested in careers as engineers.
Housing:	12th grade participants are housed in the dormitories; meal tickets for the student union cafeteria are provided for all students.
Costs:	None
Credits Given:	None
Contact:	Edmund Tellez
	Pre-engineering Summer Workshops for Women and Minorities
	University of Arizona
	College of Engineering and Mines
	Harshbarger Building # 11, Rm. 134
	Tucson, AZ 85721
	(520) 621-8103; FAX (520) 621-9995

PREFACE

Participants spend an enjoyable week on Purdue's campus while exploring the career opportunities that exist in the field of engineering. Students learn the importance of high school preparation for college, develop better study skills and learning techniques, and engage in discussions about college and life planning. The field of engineering is explored through discussions with practicing engineers and engineering students, through tours, and by hands-on activities. Each participant designs and builds at least one engineering-related project during the week. Special sessions focus on engineering as a career choice for minority students. PREFACE students also have use of the Recreational Gymnasium, which provides facilities for a number of sports activities, and participate in other leisure activities. *Application deadline: May 28.*

Host School:	Purdue University
Type:	Engineering
Location:	West Lafayette, IN
Duration:	One week
Dates:	Mid-July
Qualifications:	Entering grades 10 and 11. Open to minority students interested in exploring career opportunities in engineering. Program is limited to African American, American Indian, Mexican American, and Puerto Rican students.
Housing:	Participants are housed in the residence halls and have meals in the residence hall's dining facility.
Costs:	$100.
Credits Given:	None
Contact:	PREFACE
	Purdue University
	Minority Engineering Program
	Enad # 214
	West Lafayette, IN 47907-1286
	(317) 494-3974; FAX (317) 494-5819

Preface Program

The Preface Program is designed to provide women and minority students, traditionally underrepresented in science and engineering, an opportunity to explore possible career opportunities in the field of engineering. Participants experience problem solving on a college level and do intensive work in interactive computer graphics and computing. Lectures, laboratory experimentation, field trips, and discussions all combine to give participants a realistic look at the challenges that are part of engineering study. Career exploration activities provide a look at a future as an engineer. Evening workshops address topics that include academic planning, assessment of strengths and weaknesses, and college admissions and financial aid. *Application deadline: mid-March.*

Host School:	Rensselaer Polytechnic Institute
Type:	Engineering
Location:	Troy, NY
Duration:	Two weeks
Dates:	Middle to end of July
Qualifications:	Entering grade 12. Open to academically talented minority and women students interested in exploring careers in engineering. Participation is limited to United States citizens or permanent residents.
Housing:	Participants are housed in the university dormitories and have meals provided in the dining hall. Students have access to the campus recreational, sports, and social events.
Costs:	None. Round-trip transportation is also provided.
Credits Given:	None
Contact:	Mark Smith
	Preface Program
	Rensselaer Polytechnic Institute
	Office of Minority Student Affairs
	Troy Building
	Troy, NY 12180-3590
	(518) 276-8197

Program for Women in Science and Engineering (PWSE): Summer High School Research Internships for Women

The Program for Women in Science and Engineering (PWSE) provides young women interested in possible careers in the sciences and/or engineering with the opportunity to participate in a paid research internship under the guidance of a faculty researcher on the Iowa State University campus. Students are assigned to a mentor in their area of interest and conduct research on specific projects. A research paper and a poster summarizing the summer's work is presented by each student at a formal ceremony at the conclusion of the program. Weekly seminars organized by PWSE and optional recreational activities provide both fun experiences and a close look at the career opportunities for women that exist in the field of science and engineering. *Application deadline: February 28.*

Host School:	Iowa State University
Type:	Science and Engineering Internships
Location:	Ames, IA
Duration:	Six weeks
Dates:	Mid-June through late July
Qualifications:	Entering grade 12. Open to young women interested in science and engineering.
Housing:	Participants are housed in the residence hall and have meals in the dining facilities.
Costs:	Students are paid a stipend of $1,100. The stipend should cover transportation, room and board, and incidental personal expenses.
Credits Given:	None
Contact:	Program for Women in Science and Engineering
	Iowa State University
	210 Lab of Mechanics
	Ames, IA 50011-2130
	(515) 294-9964; FAX (515) 294-8627

Project C.A.V.E.S.

Project C.A.V.E.S. (Creative and Valuable Experiences through Spelunking) provides students with an awareness of the scientific, ecological, social, and aesthetic uses and benefits of caves and helps participants to understand how these benefits relate to the world around them. Classroom instruction at Jasper High School includes sessions on cave geology, biology, surveying, spelunking skills, and cave conservation. Students then apply what they have learned during numerous field trips to caves in the Jasper area. Some of the trips are to caves in wild, undeveloped areas; these trips are physically demanding. Project C.A.V.E.S. is presented as part of the AEGIS (Academic Enrichment for the Gifted in Summer) program. **Contact program director for application deadline.**

Host School:	Jasper School District
Type:	Cave Study
Location:	Jasper, AR
Duration:	Three weeks
Dates:	Mid-June through early July
Qualifications:	Entering grades 9 and 10. Open to Arkansas students interested in spelunking (cave exploration).
Housing:	Participants are housed in the Jasper area and are provided with meals.
Costs:	No cost to participants.
Credits Given:	None
Contact:	Jeff Middleton
	Project C.A.V.E.S.
	Jasper School District
	P.O. Box 446
	Jasper, AR 72641
	(501) 446-2223

Project G.O. (Geological Orientation)

In this unique science experience, students use geology as a way to learn about the basic fundamentals of scientific investigation, critical thought, and independent perspective. Project G.O. is a traveling geology program, taking its participants nearly 2000 miles around the state. The program covers all of Arkansas' major physiographic provinces. Students explore, discuss, study, and sample the important examples of geologic features and mineral resources found in each province. Participants keep a journal of their experiences, experiments, observations, and thoughts as they work their way around the state. Project G.O. is part of the AEGIS (Academic Enrichment for the Gifted in Summer) program. *Contact program coordinator for application deadline.*

Host School:	Crowley's Ridge ESC
Type:	Geology Field Experience
Location:	Program members travel throughout Arkansas.
Duration:	Two weeks
Dates:	Mid-July
Qualifications:	Entering grades 9 through 11. Open to Arkansas students interested in geology and scientific investigation.
Housing:	Students on this traveling program spend most nights camping out. Area motels house participants on remaining nights. All meals are provided.
Costs:	None
Credits Given:	None
Contact:	Kay Luter
	Project G.O.
	Crowley's Ridge ESC
	P.O. Box 377
	Harrisburg, AR 72432
	(501) 578-5426

Project Learning Arkansas' Natural Divisions (L.A.N.D.)

Project L.A.N.D. participants have a unique opportunity to question and evaluate how the Arkansas environment is currently being managed. L.A.N.D. students spend three weeks touring Arkansas, exploring each of the six physiographic divisions in depth through activities that include camping, hiking, canoeing, and fossil digging. Students meet with area residents and with experts in the fields of ecology, geology, cultural and physical geography, wildlife management, and botany, to gain an understanding of the land and its use. Participants take part in rigorous physical activity and need to be in excellent physical condition. This unique program is presented as part of the AEGIS (Academic Enrichment for the Gifted in Summer) program. *Contact program director or the State Department of Education, Gifted and Talented Division, for application deadline.*

Host School:	O.U.R. (The Ozark Unlimited Educational Resource Cooperative)
Type:	Environmental Science Field and Camping Experience
Location:	Students travel through the natural divisions of Arkansas
Duration:	Three weeks
Dates:	Mid-June through early July
Qualifications:	Entering grades 9 and 10. Open to physically fit Arkansas students interested in exploring the state in a unique way.
Housing:	Students spend most nights camping out in this traveling program; however, some evenings are spent in motels.
	Meals and transportation are provided.
Costs:	None
Credits Given:	None
Contact:	Roxana Wallace
	Project L.A.N.D.
	O.U.R. Education Cooperative
	665 North Star Lane
	Hector, AR 72843
	(501) 496-2336, or (501) 496-2355

Project SEE (Summer Education Experience)

Project SEE is designed to introduce students to scientific research and college-level classwork through the study of the various scientific disciplines, including biology, chemistry, geology, physical science, and computer science. Lectures are supplemented by independent research opportunities, discussions on scientific ethics, laboratory experimentation, and career exploration. Emphasis is on individual attention; the program has a faculty/student ratio of 1:4. Social, athletic, and recreational activities are available to the participants on the University of Minnesota, Morris, campus. *Application deadline: April 30.*

Host School: University of Minnesota, Morris
Type: Science
Location: Morris, MN
Duration: Seven weeks
Dates: Mid-June through the end of July
Qualifications: Entering grade 12. Open to students academically talented in the sciences as evidenced by successful completion of at least two years of science and math courses. Underrepresented minority students, women students, and physically or economically disadvantaged students are especially encouraged to apply.
Housing: Participants are housed in a residence hall and have meals in the dining hall.
Costs: No cost for tuition or housing. A cash stipend to cover all food and some personal expenses is also provided.
Credits Given: None
Contact: Thomas McRoberts
Project SEE
University of Minnesota, Morris
231 Community Services Building
Morris, MN 56267
(612) 589-6450

Protecting the Future of Ourtown:
The Role of Science and Engineering

This University of Oklahoma Summer Academy focuses on an understanding of the scientific and technical issues that confront a small, economically stressed, hypothetical town, "Ourtown." Ourtown is the site of an abandoned refinery, a lead smelter, and a proposed hazardous waste processing facility. Students explore the problems confronting the town in this simulation that allows them to assume roles of environmental professionals, homeowners, business leaders, activists, and government. Faculty members provide students with instructional experiences, and professional scientists and engineers serve as guest speakers to ensure that students gain the technical background needed to consider all aspects of the simulation. Technical sessions focus on air quality management, hazardous waste, water supplies, environmental impact assessment, and health-risk assessment. Field trips to area facilities give students a close look at real-world applications and environmental occupations. Participants come away with an understanding of how math, chemistry, biology, English, and geography relate to the skills needed to protect our environment. Special cultural, social, and recreational activities are planned for evenings and weekends. *Application deadline: April 1.*

Host School:	University of Oklahoma
Type:	Environmental Science
Location:	Norman, OK
Duration:	Three weeks
Dates:	Late June through the beginning of July
Qualifications:	Entering grades 11 and 12. Open to Oklahoma residents interested in a challenging summer experience.
Housing:	Participants are housed in dormitories and have meals in the cafeteria.
Costs:	None. Students receive a small stipend at the conclusion of the program.
Credits Given:	None
Contact:	Protecting the Future of Ourtown
	University of Oklahoma
	Precollegiate Programs: Summer Academy
	1700 Asp Avenue
	Norman, OK 73037-0001
	(405) 325-6897; FAX (405) 325-7679

Recruitment into Engineering of High-Ability Minority Students (REHAMS)

This program seeks to offer academically talented minority students a chance to experience the activities and thinking processes characteristic of engineering. This enrichment program includes classes in math, computer usage, and oral and written communication skills. Methods of solving engineering problems are presented. Participants are introduced to the various engineering disciplines by faculty members working in each of eight fields, including such areas of specialization as chemical and electrical engineering. Engineers from industry and government also talk to students about engineering opportunities for minorities. Field trips to area facilities are planned one day a week. Participants are also involved in projects that require the application of engineering principles and individual innovations. *Application deadline: March 31.*

Host School:	Louisiana State University
Type:	Engineering
Location:	Baton Rouge, LA
Duration:	Four weeks
Dates:	June
Qualifications:	Entering grade 12. Open to minority students who have outstanding high school grades in math and science and high-achievement test scores.
Housing:	Participants are housed in a residence hall and are provided with daily meals, excluding weekends.
Costs:	None with the exception of weekend meals.
Credits Given:	None
Contact:	Mrs. Forest Smith
	Recruitment into Engineering of High-Ability Minority Students
	Louisiana State University
	3304 CEBA
	College of Engineering
	Baton Rouge, LA 70803-6401
	(504) 388-5731; FAX (504) 388-5990

The Regional Center for Mathematics and Science: Health Sciences Emphasis

The Regional Center for Mathematics and Science provides science-oriented students whose parents did not graduate from a four-year college or university the chance to experience life as a college student while exploring career opportunities in the health sciences. The academic program consists of classroom instruction in math and science each weekday morning. Reading, composition, and study skill instruction are integrated into these classes. Students also participate in faculty-directed projects in the university's biology, chemistry, and physics laboratories. Students work in the computer lab three times per week, learning simple and complex programming skills, working on computer graphic designs, and using computers to do mathematical computations. Numerous field trips provide the students with ample opportunity to observe science and math in applied settings; students visit medical facilities, research labs, utilities, businesses, and industries. All day trips take participants to science education centers, while one week of the program is reserved for a field experience at the Hunt-Hill Audubon Sanctuary. Two series of personal development workshops focus on college preparation and careers and issues involved with value clarification and personal growth. A full range of recreational and sports activities complete the program. ***Application deadline: mid-April.***

Host School:	University of Wisconsin, Green Bay
Type:	Health Sciences
Location:	Green Bay, WI
Duration:	Six weeks
Dates:	Mid-June through the end of July
Qualifications:	Entering grades 10 through 12. Open to potential first-generation college students who are motivated to follow a rigorous academic program, have a minimum GPA of 2.3 (on a 4.0 scale), and are United States citizens or permanent residents.
Housing:	Participants are housed in dormitories and have meals in the dining halls.
Costs:	None. Students receive a weekly stipend of $15.
Credits Given:	High school credit may be earned.
Contact:	Scott Ashmann The Regional Center for Mathematics and Science University of Wisconsin, Green Bay 2420 Nicolet Drive, SS 1929 Green Bay, WI 54311-7001 (414) 465-2671; FAX (414) 465-2765

Research Apprentice Program in Applied Sciences

The Research Apprentice Program in Applied Sciences provides students interested in the scientific aspects of agriculture and animal health with the opportunity to receive both advanced academic instruction and laboratory research experience. Students take classes in mathematics, microcomputer applications, and communications during the academic enrichment portion of the program. Participants also spend much of their time working in the laboratory under the guidance of a research scientist from the Colleges of Agriculture and Veterinary Medicine. Seminars, field trips, and tours all provide students with a firsthand look at possible careers in applied science. ***Contact the program coordinator for application deadline.***

Host School:	University of Illinois, Champaign-Urbana
Type:	Agriculture and Veterinary Medicine Study and Internship
Location:	Champaign, IL
Duration:	Six weeks
Dates:	Late June through the end of July
Qualifications:	Entering grade 12. Open to students from populations traditionally under-represented in the sciences, including African Americans, Native Americans, Hispanic Americans, and women.
Housing:	Participants are housed in a dormitory and have meals in the dining facilities.
Costs:	None. A stipend is also provided.
Credits Given:	None
Contact:	Dr. Jesse Thompson, Jr.
	Research Apprentice Program in Applied Sciences
	University of Illinois, Champaign-Urbana
	Office of Continuing Education & Public Service
	302 E. John Street, Suite 202
	Champaign, IL 61820
	(217) 333-3380

Research Science Institute

The Research Science Institute offers its participants six of the most intellectually stimulating weeks of their lives. During the first week, on-campus morning classes focus on the newest developments in mathematics, physical and biological sciences, and the humanities. Afternoons are spent learning the technical skills needed for scientific research, including computer skills, quantitative research methods, and design. The next four weeks are spent in off-campus internships under the guidance of mentors. Projects focus on math, biology, engineering, or physical science at research sites at the Massachusetts Institute of Technology (MIT), Harvard, and other facilities in the Boston area. Students make oral and written presentations during the last week of the program. Many participants enter the Westinghouse Talent Search. *Application deadline: February 1.*

Host School:	Massachusetts Institute of Technology
Type:	Science Study/Internship
Location:	Cambridge, MA
Duration:	Six weeks
Dates:	Late June through early August
Qualifications:	Entering grade 12. Open to outstanding students who have demonstrated superior achievement in math, science, and verbal skills. Requires math PSAT of 70 and total PSAT of 135.
Housing:	Participants are housed in the dormitories and have meals in the dining halls.
Costs:	None
Credits Given:	None
Contact:	Ms. Maite Ballestero
	Research Science Institute
	The Center for Excellence in Education
	7710 Old Springhouse Road, Suite 1000
	McLean, VA 22102
	(703) 448-9062; FAX (703) 442-9513

Science Transition Program

Supported by The National Science Foundation and several corporate sponsors, Science Transition seeks those students who show a high potential for science studies but who are not the top scholars in their classes at this time. It is believed that these are students who may, with the right environment and encouragement, grow to meet their potential. The program consists of an interdisciplinary exploration of the worlds of ecology, space, marine science, and human life seen from the perspectives of biology, chemistry, earth science, and physics. Other features of the program include a mentoring program, matching individual participants with role models. A support program for parents helps them encourage their children to improve their study habits. Women and minority students are especially encouraged to apply. ***Application deadline: May 15.***

Host School:	Central Connecticut State University
Type:	Science
Location:	New Britain, CT
Duration:	Three weeks
Dates:	End of June through mid-July
Qualifications:	Entering grades 9 and 10. Open to Connecticut, Massachusetts, and Rhode Island students who exhibit a high potential for science studies but who are not currently achieving at their ability level.
Housing:	Participants are housed in residence halls and have meals in the dining hall.
Costs:	Minimal registration fee.
Credits Given:	None
Contact:	Dr. Leeds M. Carluccio
	Science Transition Program
	Central Connecticut State University
	Department of Biological Sciences
	1615 Stanley Street
	New Britain, CT 06050
	(203) 827-7279; FAX (203) 832-2946

Scientific Discovery Program— Young Scholars/PREP Program

This unusual program allows participants to experience the chemical, biological, social science, mathematical, statistical, and computer science disciplines. Laboratory work, demonstrations, lectures, and field trips illustrate their relationship to the field of water quality and solid waste management. As students acquire knowledge and skills, they apply their learning to group research projects that have both environmental and social significance in their home communities. After the institute concludes, the students have the option to continue their work at home with the help of SCSU faculty and local teachers. Other features of the program include the opportunity to shadow a working scientist or university professor and special evening presentations. Recreational activities, including an all-day canoe trip on the Mississippi River, are also featured. **Application deadline: May 3.**

Host School:	St. Cloud State University (SCSU)
Type:	Environmental Science and Waste Management
Location:	St. Cloud, MN
Duration:	Five weeks
Dates:	Mid-July through mid-August
Qualifications:	Entering grades 9, 10, and 11. Open to high-ability, high-potential students with a strong interest in science and/or mathematics. Minority and women students are especially encouraged to apply.
Housing:	Participants are housed in the dormitories and have meals in the dining hall.
Costs:	No program costs. Limited financial aid for needy students is available.
Credits Given:	None
Contact:	Dr. Robert Johnson
	Scientific Discovery Program
	St. Cloud State University
	EB B 120A
	720 Fourth Avenue, South
	St. Cloud, MN 56301-4498
	(612) 255-4928; FAX (612) 255-4237

Space Science Activities Workshop

This unusual program provides students interested in space science with an opportunity to learn about the field, perform experiments, and explore career opportunities in this area. The workshop is an interdisciplinary study of related sciences, and presents numerous opportunities for students to take part in hands-on discovery activities. Some of the activities include experiments at an amusement park; others involve hot-air balloons and a microgravity simulation in a swimming pool. Field trips, equipment construction, use of NASA materials and computer software are supplemented by evening observational astronomy and scuba diving. Secondary school science teachers team with students to test materials for use in their home schools. ***Application deadline: April 27.***

Host School:	University of Northern Iowa
Type:	Space Science
Location:	Cedar Falls, IA
Duration:	Two weeks
Dates:	Middle through late July
Qualifications:	Entering grades 10 through 12. Students should have a demonstrated interest in science, and at least a 2.0 grade point average.
Housing:	Participants are housed in the dormitory and have meals in the dining hall.
Costs:	$100. Travel expenses are also provided.
Credits Given:	None
Contact:	Space Science Activities Workshop
	University of Northern Iowa
	Physics Department
	Cedar Falls, IA 50614-0150
	FAX: (319) 273-5813

Summer Computer Program

Middle school students interested in computers have the opportunity to take part in this exciting program that combines hands-on study with the latest in computer technology. Additional exposure to other areas of science, industrial tours, and discussions about scientific ethics and policy complete the program. Students begin work on individual and group projects that are continued during the coming school year. Teams present the results of their work to the entire group. Project advisers remain in contact with each student and may visit the student's school for a supplemental presentation. All participants and staff attend a two-day follow-up conference early in the following summer. Field trips, tours, and talks by visiting computer professionals provide students with a close look at opportunities for computer careers. Students may use the campus's sports and recreational facilities to enjoy activities such as bowling, tennis, and swimming. Computer science majors at the university act as assistants during this program and live in the residence halls with the students. *Application deadline: May 7.*

Host School:	Northeast Louisiana University
Type:	Computer Science
Location:	Monroe, LA
Duration:	Three weeks
Dates:	Early through late June
Qualifications:	Entering grades 8 and 9. Open to high-ability and high-potential students interested in computer science, mathematics, or science. Women, minority students, and handicapped students are especially encouraged to apply.
Housing:	Participants are housed in dormitories located near the Computer Center and have meals in the dining hall.
Costs:	None. A special fund is available to provide travel expenses for needy students.
Credits Given:	None
Contact:	Dr. Virginia Eaton
	Summer Computer Program
	Northeast Louisiana University
	Department of Computer Science
	Monroe, LA 71209-0575
	(318) 342-1848

Summer Engineering Academy (SEA): Minority Introduction to Technology and Engineering (MITE)

Each of the summer minority student programs in engineering at the University of Michigan focuses on academic enrichment in mathematics, computers, technical communications, and engineering concepts. In the intensive MITE program, participants study the academic core subjects listed and have the opportunity to interact with engineering role models through field trips, speakers, and other enrichment activities. Guidance sessions focus on preparation for college, college admissions, financial aid, and the skills needed for academic and professional success. ***Application deadline: April 30.***

Host School:	University of Michigan
Type:	Engineering and Technology
Location:	Ann Arbor, MI
Duration:	Two weeks
Dates:	Late July through late August
Qualifications:	Entering grades 8 through 12. The program is directed toward minority students (African Americans, Hispanics, and Native Americans) who are interested in exploring the world of engineering and its career opportunities. Participants must have completed Algebra I.
Housing:	Participants are housed in dormitories and have meals in the dining halls.
Costs:	None
Credits Given:	None
Contact:	Summer Engineering Academy (SEA): Minority Introduction to Technology
	University of Michigan
	Minority Engineering Program Office (MEPO)
	1301 Beal Avenue, 2316 EECS Building
	Ann Arbor, MI 48109-2116
	(313) 764-6497

Summer Engineering Academy (SEA): Summer Apprenticeship Program (SAP)

The Summer Apprenticeship Program places interested students with engineering faculty and graduate-level assistants conducting research projects in one of the engineering disciplines. SAP allows students to get hands-on experience while they develop research skills, giving students an extensive practical view of the field of engineering. A Student Technical Symposium, at which students present the results of their research experience, is held at the end of the apprenticeship program and provides students with a look at ongoing research in other engineering disciplines. *Application deadline: April 30.*

Host School:	University of Michigan
Type:	Engineering Internship
Location:	Ann Arbor, MI
Duration:	Eight weeks
Dates:	Late June through mid-August
Qualifications:	Entering grades 11 and 12. Open to minority students (African American, Hispanic, and Native American) interested in practical experience in engineering. Program is nonresidential; only students able to commute to and from the University of Michigan campus each day are considered.
Housing:	Housing is not available.
Costs:	None. Students may either receive a stipend for their work or may earn high school credit.
Credits Given:	High school credit may be available.
Contact:	Summer Engineering Academy (SEA): Summer Apprenticeship Program University of Michigan Minority Engineering Program Office (MEPO) 1301 Beal Avenue, 2316 EECS Building Ann Arbor, MI 48109-2116 (313) 764-6497

Summer Engineering Academy (SEA):
Summer College Engineering Exposure Program (SCEEP)

Along with the other programs offered by SEA at the University of Michigan, SCEEP focuses on academic enrichment in mathematics, computer science, technical communications, and engineering concepts. This program, in particular, exposes participants to the university environment and explores the various engineering majors offered by the College of Engineering. Students participate in departmental tours and interact with faculty and staff, current students, and alumni. Campus tours and activities help the students feel at home on the University of Michigan campus and acquaint them with college life. Special workshops address academic skills needed for success, college admissions, the financial aid process, and available support services. *Application deadline: April 30.*

Host School:	University of Michigan
Type:	Introduction to Engineering, Mathematics, and Computer Science
Location:	Ann Arbor, MI
Duration:	One week
Dates:	Two sessions held during the second and third weeks of August.
Qualifications:	Entering grades 11 and 12. Open to minority students (African Americans, Hispanics, and Native Americans) interested in possible majors in engineering.
Housing:	Participants are housed in the dormitories and have meals in the dining halls.
Costs:	No cost to participants.
Credits Given:	None
Contact:	Summer Engineering Academy (SEA): Summer College Engineering Exposure Program
	University of Michigan
	Minority Engineering Program Office (MEPO)
	1301 Beal Avenue, 2316 EECS Building
	Ann Arbor, MI 48109-2116
	(313) 764-6497

Summer Minority Student Science Training Program

Alabama A & M sponsors a variety of student science programs, both residential and commuter, supported by the National Science Foundation. The elementary and middle school programs (students grades 5 through 9) are for commuter students only; the high school programs serve both commuter and residential students. Students in the Research Participation (internship) Program are involved in research experiences which provide information about modern trends in science, mathematics, and engineering disciplines, as well as an understanding of career opportunities. The goal of the Science Training Program is to provide science research and/or enrichment experiences to motivate minority students to consider a career in science and engineering. *Application deadline: April 15.*

Host School:	Alabama A & M University
Type:	Science Study and Internship
Location:	Normal, AL
Duration:	Five to six weeks, depending upon program chosen
Dates:	Mid-June through end of July
Qualifications:	Grades 4 through first year of college (students entering grades 11, 12, and first year of college may apply for the internship program). The program is open to minority students with a B average or better.
Housing:	Participants are housed in a dormitory and have meals in the cafeteria.
Costs:	None. Students receive stipends of $375 to $450 for the precollege program, and stipends of $1350 for first-year college program.
Credits Given:	None
Contact:	Dr. Jerry Shipman
	Summer Minority Student Science Training Program
	Alabama A & M University
	P.O. Box 326
	Normal, AL 35762
	(205) 851-5316; FAX (205) 851-5622

Summer Program in Marine Science

This innovative program for hearing-impaired high school students is held on the campus of the Marine Science Consortium at Wallops Island, Virginia. Through lectures, laboratory work, and field trips, students explore the world of marine science. Students may explore coastal, beach, and marsh ecology; shipboard and oceanographic techniques; animal behavior; marine biology; and other related areas. Field trips to the National Aquarium in Baltimore, to NASA rocket operations, to the National Oceanic and Atmospheric Administration's weather station, and to the Assateague National Wildlife Refuge give students a view of existing science and career opportunities in the marine sciences. In addition to group experiences, each student completes a research project under the supervision of a faculty member. Recreational activities and evening hours are supervised by resident recreational counselors. ***Application deadline: May 10.***

Host School:	Marine Science Consortium—West Virginia University
Type:	Marine Science
Location:	Wallops Island, VA
Duration:	Four weeks
Dates:	Late June through late July
Qualifications:	Entering grades 9 through 12. Open to highly motivated hearing-impaired students interested in hands-on study of marine science.
Housing:	Faculty, counselors, and students are housed together in the dormitory on the campus of the Marine Science Consortium. Meals are served in the cafeteria.
Costs:	Student stipends cover all costs of the program.
Credits Given:	None
Contact:	Dr. Joseph Marshall
	Summer Program in Marine Science
	Marine Science Consortium—West Virginia University
	Department of Biology
	P.O. Box 6057
	Morgantown, WV 26506-6057
	(304) 293-5201; FAX (304) 293-6363

Student Profile

Tosha Wheeler
Ste. Genevieve, Mo.
Summer Program
in Marine Science
Tosha, 17, attends the Missouri School for the Deaf in Fulton, Mo. She has attended science enrichment programs for the past few summers.

Hello, my name is Tosha Wheeler. I live in Ste. Genevieve, Missouri. In the summer of 1994, I went to Marine Science Consortium in Wallop's Island, Virginia, for Marine Biology Camp. I stayed at the camp for four weeks learning about marine biology and different areas in science. We went on trips to learn about animal life and different majors in Marine Biology. Several places that we visited were NASA, the Sea Aquarium in Baltimore, Maryland, and the Crab House to see how they get crab meat and send it off to the market.

Once each week, our group went out to the ocean to collect animals. We did that by trawling. We had a trawling net and threw it out into the ocean and waited for approximately ten minutes before we hauled the net back in.

After we collected animals, we took them back to our lab and each of us picked an animal to do a research project on. I picked Spider Crabs (Libiniz) for my research project. Libiniz is the scientific name for spider crabs. I had to find out about its background and its habitat. I got all my research information together and put it on posterboard and presented it before my group, counselors, and teachers.

I liked this experience because this camp let me work hands-on with animals, which I didn't get to do in the classroom at school. The most fascinating thing about it is that we got to go out into the ocean and collect animals for ourselves.

If we didn't have programs like this one, I never would have the chance to experience these things firsthand. It has influenced my decision about what I would like to do in the future.

Summer Research Training Program: Physiology and Biochemistry of Microorganisms

Students interested in a research experience have the opportunity to work with Pace University upperclassmen who have participated in their undergraduate research program. Students are taught basic microbial techniques and perform experiments involving a variety of microorganisms. Students who have had previous exposure to microbiology are assigned to an advanced group. These students experiment with cutting DNA with restriction endonucleases, heredity unit transfer, and incorporation of plasmids. Students who continue with their studies after the six-week program have the opportunity to develop their own research studies. These studies often are appropriate for participation in science fairs and the Westinghouse competition. *Application deadline: March 31.*

Host School:	Pace University
Type:	Science Study and Internship
Location:	New York, NY
Duration:	Six weeks
Dates:	Early July through late August
Qualifications:	Entering grades 11 and 12. Directed to students with a strong interest in the biological and biochemical sciences. Students who belong to groups underrepresented in the sciences are especially welcome.
Housing:	This is mainly a commuter program, although dormitory housing can be arranged for students needing these accommodations.
Costs:	None except for lunch and travel expenses.
Credits Given:	None
Contact:	Dr. Dudley Cox
	Pace University
	Department of Biological Sciences
	1 Pace Plaza
	New York, NY 10038
	(212) 346-1504

Summer Scientific Seminar

This program offers participants a unique opportunity to get a firsthand look at academic and student life at the United States Air Force Academy. Students choose from a wide variety of scientific seminars focusing on topics such as metaphysics, astronomy, geopolitics, computer-aided drawing, electronics, field biology, airmanship, and technical writing. Tours of the laboratories and flight line are also available to the participants. Current cadets host and escort students, providing guidance and information about life as a cadet. Students can also explore the opportunities available to scientists and engineers in the Air Force. Evening programs include informational sessions and athletic and recreational activities. *Application deadline: early February.*

Host School:	United States Air Force Academy
Type:	Science
Location:	Golden, CO
Duration:	One week
Dates:	Two sessions: Mid-June and late June.
Qualifications:	Entering grade 12. Open to students interested in becoming Air Force Academy cadets. Applicants must be ranked in the top third of their class and have minimum scores of at least 50 verbal, 55 math on the PSAT (500 verbal and 550 math on SAT), or composite of 24 on the PACT.
Housing:	Participants are housed in a cadet dormitory and have meals in the dining hall.
Costs:	$100 plus transportation costs to and from the Air Force Academy. Limited financial aid is available.
Credits Given:	None
Contact:	Summer Scientific Seminar United States Air Force Academy HQ USAFA / RRMX 2304 Cadet Drive, Suite 211 USAF Academy, CO 80840-5025 (719) 472-2236

$\mathbf{S}$OARS: Space Opportunities and Research Summer

Students interested in space-related topics can spend an exciting two weeks working with engineers and scientists in their laboratories at the Penn State Space Grant Consortium. Participants engage in challenging research that includes study of black holes, the origins of the universe, the effects of weightlessness, and changing patterns of the world's ecosystems. Daily discussions about research and careers are led by practicing scientists, engineers, and mathematicians. Students tour laboratories conducting space-related research and use the libraries to read about the newest advances. Free time may be spent using Penn State's athletic facilities (including both the swimming pool and ice rink), and taking part in informal discussions. ***Application deadline: early March.***

Host School:	Penn State University
Type:	Space Science Internship
Location:	University Park, PA
Duration:	Two weeks
Dates:	Late June through early July
Qualifications:	Entering grades 11 and 12. Open to high-achieving and high-potential students. Students should have strong grades and have completed a course in algebra II. Female, minority, and disabled students are strongly encouraged to apply.
Housing:	Participants are housed in residence halls and are provided with meals.
Costs:	None. Some travel funds are available for students in need.
Credits Given:	None
Contact:	Dr. Richard Devon
	SOARS Program
	Penn State University
	102 S. Frear Lab
	University Park, PA 16802
	(814) 863-7688; FAX (814) 863-8286

Summer Study in Engineering Program for High School Women

The program seeks to expose young women to a program of college-level engineering study. With this exposure they will have the knowledge needed to make an informed decision about a possible career in engineering. The sponsors also hope to provide the students with the confidence that they can be successful in engineering study. Participants take two courses: Introductory Engineering Science provides an introduction to engineering science and design, including the use of computers to solve engineering problems. Computer applications are stressed and the students work as a group to design, manufacture, and assemble a project. The World of Engineering serves as an introduction to the various engineering disciplines. Students spend time in each engineering department, visiting laboratories, and completing exercises typical of each field of engineering. Field trips and visits complement this experience.

Application deadline: May 15.

Host School:	University of Maryland
Type:	Engineering
Location:	College Park, MD
Duration:	Six weeks
Dates:	Mid-July through late August
Qualifications:	Entering grade 12. Open to women interested in engineering as a possible career choice. Admission is competitive.
Housing:	Participants are strongly encouraged to live in university housing and have meals in the dining hall.
Costs:	None for instruction and housing. Students are responsible for the cost of their meals.
Credits Given:	Six college credits
Contact:	Summer Study in Engineering Program for High School Women
	University of Maryland
	College of Engineering
	1131 Engineering Classroom Building
	College Park, MD 20742
	(301) 405-3936; FAX (301) 314-9867

Summer Ventures in Science and Math (SVSM)

A statewide program of the University of North Carolina system, Summer Ventures in Science and Mathematics (SVSM) is administered by the North Carolina School of Science and Mathematics. Six campuses host the SVSM Institutes, each with different programs. The academic program is designed to provide students with experience in scientific inquiry and mathematical problem solving. Students develop laboratory skills and study experimental design, instrumentation, mathematical modeling and problem solving, and data analysis. A research topic of individual interest fills the remaining study period. Computer applications, career guidance, and discussions about social issues are also part of the summer program. Applications may be obtained through North Carolina high school guidance counseling offices beginning in mid-October. *Application deadline: January 31.*

Host School: North Carolina School of Science and Mathematics

Type: Science and Mathematics

Location: Six campuses including UNC at Charlotte, UNC at Wilmington, Appalachian State, Eastern Carolina University, Western Carolina University, and North Carolina Central University.

Duration: Four weeks

Dates: Two sessions: Mid-June through mid-July, early July through early August.

Qualifications: Entering grades 11 and 12. Open to North Carolina residents selected for academic ability, science and mathematics motivation, and emotional maturity.

Housing: Participants are housed in dormitories and have meals provided in the dining halls.

Costs: None. Limited funds are available to help with transportation and personal expenses for students with severe financial need.

Credits Given: None

Contact: Summer Ventures in Science and Math (SVSM)
University of North Carolina
P.O. Box 2976
Durham, NC 27715
(919) 286-3366 ext. 523

Tennessee Governor's School for the Sciences

The Governor's School program provides intensive instruction in one area of science or mathematics, teaching the methods and current ideas of practicing scientists. Classes are held Monday through Friday and Saturday morning. One of the morning sessions is devoted to the art of thinking mathematically. A writing component explores the development of ideas and effectively communicating them to others. Computing classes help students deal with volumes of data effectively. Afternoon sessions are devoted to intense study of the student's choice, emphasizing research and problem solving. Evening discussions cover philosophy, ethics, and current concerns. Social and recreational activities are also planned. ***Contact program for more information. Application deadline: December.***

Host School:	University of Tennessee, Knoxville
Type:	Science and Mathematics
Location:	Knoxville, TN
Duration:	Four weeks
Dates:	Mid-June through mid-July
Qualifications:	Entering grades 11 and 12. Open to Tennessee residents.
Housing:	Participants are housed in a dormitory and have meals in the dining hall.
Costs:	None
Credits Given:	None
Contact:	Director
	Tennessee Governor's School for the Sciences
	University of Tennessee, Knoxville
	Suite 191 Hoskins
	Knoxville, TN 37996-4120
	(615) 974-0756

Upward Bound: Cranbrook

While taking part in the Cranbrook Educational Community, students work in scientific teams, conducting research on topics such as the physics of motion, river and lake ecosystems, forest communities, and star study. Participants take accelerated classes in science and math, studying biology/ecology, research methods, and methods of generating and displaying scientific data. Field trips to area laboratories and universities allow for career exploration. Students gain confidence as they improve their oral and written communication, as well as study and research skills. Free time is for cultural and sports activities including horseback riding, canoeing, and camping. ***Application deadline: April 15.***

Host School:	Cranbrook Schools Science and Math Program
Type:	Science and Mathematics
Location:	Bloomfield Hills, MI
Duration:	Six weeks
Dates:	Late June through the end of July
Qualifications:	Entering grades 10 and 11. Applicants should be interested in science and math, have a grade point average of at least 3.0, and have completed at least one high school math and one science class. Program is open to students who will be the first in their family to attend college.
Housing:	Participants are housed in a dormitory and have meals in the dining hall.
Costs:	None. Transportation costs are also provided.
Credits Given:	None
Contact:	Upward Bound: Cranbrook
	Cranbrook Schools Science and Math Program
	1221 N. Woodward Avenue
	P.O. Box 801
	Bloomfield Hills, MI 48303-0801
	(810) 645-3676 or (810) 645-3256; FAX (810) 645-3050

Virginia Governor's School for Science and Technology

This Virginia Governor's School program focuses on the connections between science, technology, and society. The learning experience features three paths: creation of a knowledge base, experimentation, and applications related to the role of science in a global society. Students select a scientific discipline for intensive study, choosing from biology, chemistry, astronomy, mathematics/ computer science, and geology. Each student then works in this field as a member of a laboratory-based research team that includes a university professor, a graduate student, and a secondary school teacher. Students learn to apply scientific concepts to problem solving, utilizing computer modeling and other new technologies. Special seminars examine scientific ethics, moral decision making, and the history and philosophy of science. A counseling component advises students on college and career issues and on the development of social skills. Recreational, social, cultural, and sports activities complete the program. ***Contact your high school counselor, gifted coordinator, or the Department of Education for application information.***

Host School:	Hosted by a Virginia college or university
Type:	Science and Technology
Location:	Selected site in Virginia
Duration:	Four weeks
Dates:	July
Qualifications:	Entering grades 11 and 12. Open to gifted Virginia residents interested in science and technology.
Housing:	Participants are housed in residence halls and have meals in the dining facilities.
Costs:	None
Credits Given:	None
Contact:	Dr. Janie Craig
	Virginia Governor's School for Science and Technology
	Programs for the Gifted
	Department of Education
	P.O. Box 6Q
	Richmond, VA 23216-2060
	(804) 371-6880

Virginia Governor's School: Mentorship in Medicine

This Medical College of Virginia (MCV) program provides students interested in the clinical and research health sciences with the opportunity to be matched with a mentor. Each student is assigned to a physician and/or research scientist with these professionals representing a full spectrum of the health sciences. While working with their mentor, each student can observe, learn, and experience professional health science firsthand, planning and implementing individual activities. Supplementary lectures, workshops, tours, and volunteer work at the hospital give the participants an overall view of careers in the field of medicine. Time is also provided for a full complement of recreational, social, cultural, and sports activities. ***Contact the program coordinator for application deadline.***

Host School:	Medical College of Virginia
Type:	Health Sciences Internship
Location:	Richmond, VA
Duration:	Six weeks
Dates:	Late June through early August
Qualifications:	Entering grades 11 and 12. Open to outstanding Virginia students interested in the health scences.
Housing:	Participants are housed in residence halls and have meals in the dining facilities.
Costs:	None
Credits Given:	None
Contact:	David Mitnick
	Virginia Governor's School: Mentorship in Medicine
	Medical College of Virginia
	P.O. Box 565
	Richmond, VA 23298
	(804) 786-9629

Virginia Governor's School: NASA/VIMS Mentorships

The NASA/VIMS program provides interested students with the opportunity to work on a scientific research project under the guidance of professional scientists at the National Aeronautics and Space Administration (NASA) and at the Virginia Institute of Marine Science (VIMS). Students are matched with mentors, allowing the students to observe, learn, and experience space engineering or oceanographic science firsthand. These mentorships provide experiences that allow participants to develop an appreciation for scientific research and inquiry. Residential life activities, including social, recreational, athletic, and cultural components, supplement the mentorships to provide students with a well-rounded summer experience. *Contact your high school counselor, gifted coordinator, or the Department of Education for application information.*

Host School:	Hosted by a Virginia college or university
Type:	Aeronautics and Marine Science Internships
Location:	Hampton and Gloucester Point, VA
Duration:	Five weeks
Dates:	Late June through July
Qualifications:	Entering grades 11 and 12. Open to gifted Virginia residents interested in a research experience in aeronautics or marine science.
Housing:	Participants are housed in the dormitories and have meals in the dining hall.
Costs:	None
Credits Given:	None
Contact:	Dr. Janie Craig
	Virginia Governor's School: NASA/VIMS Mentorships
	Programs for the Gifted
	Department of Education
	P.O. Box 6Q
	Richmond, VA 23216-2060
	(804) 371-6880

Wet 'n Wild

Wet 'n Wild takes its participants to the Ozark Natural Science Center. Students are involved in field classes, participating in hands-on learning experiences. Students study both the organic and inorganic features of the Ozarks. These studies include: plant ecology, freshwater aquatic biology, ornithology (birds), geology (rocks and minerals), entomology (insects), ichthyology (fish), herpetology (reptiles), mammalogy (mammals), and speleology (caves). Field trips, discussions about current concerns and environmental issues, as well as opportunities to extend learnings into arts areas, round out this unusual program. Wet 'n Wild is part of the AEGIS program (Academic Enrichment for the Gifted in Summer). **Contact program coordinator for application deadline.**

Host School:	Rogers Public Schools
Type:	Ecology and Environmental Science
Location:	Rogers, AR
Duration:	Two weeks
Dates:	Late July through early August
Qualifications:	Entering grades 10 and 11. Open to Arkansas students who love the outdoors and appreciate the wonders of the natural world.
Housing:	Housing and meals are provided.
Costs:	None
Credits Given:	None
Contact:	Beth Carnes
	Wet 'n Wild
	Rogers Public Schools
	409 South 8th Street
	Rogers, AR 72756
	(501) 631-3517

The West Virginia Governor's Middle School for Science and Mathematics

West Virginia's brightest young science- and math-oriented students are invited to apply for the Governor's Middle School for Science and Mathematics. This one-week program mirrors the three-week offering for older students. Students take part in intensive morning classes, selecting studies in the science or math field of their choice. Classes include discussions, as well as laboratory experiences, that go beyond what is available to students at their home schools. Afternoon sessions are devoted to short mini-courses that focus on a particular aspect of science. Field trips to area scientific facilities and visits by practicing scientists provide students with a realistic look at the career opportunities in the sciences and mathematics. Students become familiar with the West Virginia microcomputer network and are encouraged to keep in contact with each other through the bulletin board system. A full range of recreational, social, and cultural activities completes this interesting program. ***Application deadline: February 15.***

Host School:	West Virginia University
Type:	Science and Mathematics
Location:	Morgantown, WV
Duration:	One week
Dates:	Mid-July
Qualifications:	Entering grade 8. Open to outstanding West Virginia middle school students interested in science and/or math.
Housing:	Participants are housed in a dormitory and have their meals in the dining hall.
Costs:	None
Credits Given:	None
Contact:	Dr. Virginia Simmons
	The West Virginia Governor's Middle School for Science and Mathematics
	West Virginia Department of Education
	Building 6, Room 362, Capitol Complex
	Charleston, WV 25305-0330
	(304) 558-0160; FAX (304) 558-0048

The West Virginia Governor's School for Science and Mathematics

Students at the West Virginia Governor's School for Science and Mathematics have the opportunity to engage in intensive study in a field of their choice. Morning courses find students involved in classroom discussions, laboratory experiments, and scientific research. In an unusual approach, each class consists of one faculty member, eight students, and four "teacher-participants." (The teacher-participants are experienced classroom teachers who work with, and under the direction of, the faculty members. They are encouraged to return to their home schools with the ideas and techniques learned at the Governor's School.) Afternoon courses consist of 3-day mini-courses, concentrating on one aspect of a scientific topic. Students also take part in numerous field trips visiting nearby laboratory and scientific research facilities. Computers are integrated into all of the classroom areas. All West Virginia Governor's School participants are taught to access the West Virginia microcomputer network, encouraging Governor's School participants to keep in contact. A vocational component finds guest professionals from all career areas, meeting with small groups to provide students with a close look at career opportunities. A college planning component helps students identify further study opportunities. Evenings are occupied with cultural and social activities. ***Application deadline: February 15.***

Host School:	West Virginia University
Type:	Science and Mathematics
Location:	Morgantown, WV
Duration:	Three weeks
Dates:	Late June through mid-July
Qualifications:	Entering grade 11. Open to outstanding West Virginia students interested in science and/or mathematics. Students qualify for the program by means of excellent grades and high standardized test scores.
Housing:	Participants are housed in a dormitory and have meals in the dining facilities.
Costs:	None
Credits Given:	None
Contact:	Dr. Virginia Simmons
	The West Virginia Governor's School for Science and Mathematics
	West Virginia Department of Education
	Building 6, Room 362, Capitol Complex
	Charleston, WV 25305-0330
	(304) 558-0160; FAX (304) 558-0048

Western Maryland Math Center

High-potential students excited by mathematics will be energized by this exciting weeklong program. Students are introduced to the latest in mathematics technology, through the use of computers, graphing calculators, models, and big-screen projection. The program emphasizes cooperative group experimentation, and provides enrichment experiences involving data analysis and the development of mathematical conjectures under the guidance of "master" teachers. Students experience distance learning and discover better ways to learn mathematical concepts. Upon completion of the program, participants have a better understanding of what it will take to achieve mathematical excellence as we move into the twenty-first century. *Application deadline: April 21.*

Host School:	Garrett Community College
Type:	Mathematics
Location:	McHenry, MD
Duration:	One week
Dates:	Mid-July
Qualifications:	Entering grades 7 through 9. Open to Maryland students interested in mathematics.
Housing:	Participants are housed in dormitories and have their meals in the dining hall.
Costs:	$200. Need-based financial aid is available.
Credits Given:	None
Contact:	Nancy Priselac
	Western Maryland Math Center
	Garrett Community College
	P.O. Box 151, Mosser Road
	McHenry, MD 21541

Women in Engineering and Technology

Young women interested in possibly pursuing careers in engineering and technology will find this summer program a good introduction. Students attend engineering classes and experience the applications of these principles through laboratory work. Participants work together on group design projects, challenging their creative abilities and increasing their technical skills. Visits to local industries and research centers provide students with a showcase of existing applications within technology. Special lectures by guest speakers and sessions focusing on engineering careers give women a realistic look at their opportunities. Recreational and social activities complete this informative program. ***Application deadline: June 15.***

Host School:	Ohio University
Type:	Engineering and Technology
Location:	Athens, OH
Duration:	Two weeks
Dates:	Middle through late July
Qualifications:	Entering grades 11 and 12. Open to young women interested in learning more about engineering careers who have completed at least two years of high school mathematics.
Housing:	Participants are housed in the dormitories and have meals in the dining hall.
Costs:	$150
Credits Given:	None
Contact:	Dr. Joseph Essman
	Women in Engineering and Technology
	Ohio University
	Russ College of Engineering & Technology
	150 Stocker Center
	Athens, OH 45701
	(614) 593-1482

Women in Engineering Program

This weeklong workshop provides young women with the opportunity to explore possible careers in engineering. Through laboratory work and field exercises, students explore the various engineering disciplines. These disciplines include: mechanical, civil, chemical, metallurgical, geological, and mining engineering, and some of the newer fields including bioengineering, biotechnology/forestry, engineering technology, and space science. Participants are introduced to the academic requirements necessary for engineering study and interact with professional women engineers, who also serve as role models. Cooperative education and military career opportunities are also explored. Evening presentations feature information sessions on college admissions and financial aid. The program also provides an early look at college life and includes recreational, sports, and social activities. ***Application deadline: April 8.***

Host School:	Michigan Technological University
Type:	Engineering
Location:	Houghton, MI
Duration:	One week
Dates:	Mid-June
Qualifications:	Entering grades 10 through 12. Open to young women with a strong science and math background. Participants should have completed two years of high school math and a year of chemistry.
Housing:	Participants are housed in a residence hall and have meals in the dining hall.
Costs:	$35 registration fee
Credits Given:	None
Contact:	Ms. Kerry Hicks
	Women in Engineering Program
	Michigan Technological University
	Youth Programs Office
	1400 Townsend Drive
	Houghton, MI 49931
	(906) 487-2219; FAX (906) 487-3101

Women in Science and Engineering (WISE) Summer Program

The Women in Science and Engineering (WISE) Summer Program is designed to provide young women with broader exposure to academic and career possibilities within the fields of science, engineering, and technology. Activities include college "mini-courses," laboratory experiments, panel discussions, academic and career advising, industry tours, and professional mentoring opportunities. Participants discover their own talents, learn about specific technical careers, and understand how to best prepare for college. Career opportunities for women are explored through trips to Chicago-area engineering companies and research sites, and in meetings with professional women scientists and engineers. Social and recreational activities complement the program.

Application deadline: June 1.

Host School:	Illinois Institute of Technology
Type:	Science, Engineering, and Technology
Location:	Chicago, IL
Duration:	Two weeks
Dates:	July. Two sessions are held. Session I is for students grades 9 and 10; session II is for students grades 11 and 12.
Qualifications:	Entering grades 9 through 12. Open to young women who enjoy science and mathematics and who are interested in learning about career opportunities in these fields.
Housing:	WISE participants may commute to campus or may be housed in residence halls. Meals are taken in the dining facilities.
Costs:	No cost for commuter students. $350 for room and board for students living in the college residence halls.
Credits Given:	None
Contact:	Women in Science and Engineering (WISE) Summer Program
	Illinois Institute of Technology
	71 East 32nd Street
	Women's Educational Development Center, Residence Hall
	Chicago, IL 60616
	(312) 808-7435

Women in Science and Mathematics Workshop

Designed to introduce participants to opportunities for women in the sciences, mathematics, and related research careers, this workshop joins outstanding students with professional women scientists and mathematicians. The focus is on the role of women at the cutting edge and includes presentations by speakers from industry, medicine, education, and small business. Laboratory and experimental work is performed in fields such as microbiology, molecular biology, biochemistry, forensic science, and quantitative analysis.

Application deadline: May 22.

Host School:	College of Mount St. Joseph
Type:	Science and Mathematics
Location:	Cincinnati, OH
Duration:	One week
Dates:	Mid-June
Qualifications:	Entering grades 11 and 12. Open to outstanding high school women interested in exploring opportunities in science and mathematics.
Housing:	Participants are housed in the dormitories and have meals in the dining facilities.
Costs:	$100 application fee, refundable if the student is not selected for the program.
Credits Given:	None
Contact:	Dr. G. Kritsky
	Women in Science and Mathematics Workshop
	College of Mount St. Joseph
	Department of Biology
	Cincinnati, OH 45233-1670
	(513) 244-4411; FAX (513) 244-4222

Young Scholars Program: Engineering Summer Program

Students selected for this Young Scholars Program explore the field of engineering through practical experiences. Participants can choose to build a digital circuit, to design building trusses, test the aerodynamics of a tennis racket, or study acid rain. The areas of materials science, computer-aided engineering, and environmental engineering issues are explored. Students work closely with faculty members who challenge their imagination, and develop creative thinking and problem-solving skills. Seminars on college admissions and career awareness expand the participants' knowledge. Field trips to engineering facilities, along with cultural, recreational, and social events round out the program. *Application deadline: April 15.*

Host School:	University of Wyoming
Type:	Engineering
Location:	Laramie, WY
Duration:	Three weeks
Dates:	June
Qualifications:	Entering grade 12. Students should be interested in hands-on experience in the various fields of engineering. Selection is competitive.
Housing:	Participants are housed in a residence hall and have meals in the dining facilities.
Costs:	$25 activity fee. For students with unusual financial need, an additional stipend may be provided.
Credits Given:	None
Contact:	Susan McCormack
	Young Scholars Program: Engineering Summer Program
	University of Wyoming
	College of Engineering, Box 3295
	Laramie, WY 82071
	(307) 766-4254; FAX (307) 766-4444

Young Scholars Program:
Exploration of Careers in Science

This program provides an exploration of science careers by combining two weeks of study with six weeks of research participation. Participants are introduced to research methodology, explore current topics in science, and consider ethical issues through lectures, demonstrations, field trips and tours, and laboratory experiments. After two weeks exploring fields such as astronomy, anthropology, geology, math, optometry, physics, and psychology, participants are assigned to research teams in the student's area of interest, conducting research under the guidance of a mentor scientist. Presentation of research results concludes this section of the program. Students also have the opportunity to participate in an anthropological dig and enjoy recreational and social programs. *Application deadline: April 1.*

Host School:	Indiana University
Type:	Science Study and Internship
Location:	Bloomington, IN
Duration:	Eight weeks
Dates:	Mid-June through mid-August
Qualifications:	Entering grades 11 and 12. Open to Indiana high school students who have an interest in science or mathematics, and a G.P.A. of at least 3.0.
Housing:	Participants are housed in a dormitory and have meals in the dining facilities.
Costs:	None. All participants earn a $600 stipend plus $100 travel costs. Needy students may apply for larger stipends.
Credits Given:	None
Contact:	Young Scholars Program: Exploration of Careers in Science
	Indiana University
	College of Arts and Sciences
	Kirkwood Hall #207
	Bloomington, IN 47405
	(812) 855-5397; FAX (812) 855-2060

Young Scholars Program in Coastal Erosion and Preservation

Students explore coastal erosion on a Gulf of Mexico beach and follow up their field discoveries with laboratory and classroom work. Each year our nation's coastline erodes still more; Louisiana loses 60 square miles of land to the ocean each year. Participants in this Young Scholars Program discover some of the reasons for this occurrence and explore ways to use engineering technology to solve the problem. Participants spend time on Holly Beach, the site of an outdoor laboratory, to study erosion and coastal preservation. Students work in the laboratories using wave tanks and build and test their own coastal protection devices. Classwork and a three-day field trip to one of the finest coastal engineering laboratories in the world complete the program. *Application deadline: April 15.*

Host School:	McNeese State University
Type:	Engineering
Location:	Lake Charles, LA
Duration:	Three weeks
Dates:	Two sessions are held: middle to late June and early to late July.
Qualifications:	Entering grades 10 through 12. Selection is based on records, recommendations, and an essay.
	Participants are housed in a dormitory and have most meals in the cafeteria.
Housing:	Students are provided with an $10 per day meal allowance when off campus.
Costs:	None. Financial aid is available for students who need help with transportation expenses.
Credits Given:	None
Contact:	Mary Richardson
	Young Scholars Program in Coastal Erosion and Preservation
	McNeese State University
	P.O. Box 90215
	Lake Charles, LA 70609
	(318) 475-5123; FAX (318) 475-5122

Young Scholars Program in Computing

Students in this National Science Foundation–sponsored program are introduced to the science of computing through formal instruction, laboratory activities, and field trips. Hands-on experiences coupled with exposure to working professionals provide participants with a clear view of career opportunities in the field of computer technology. Students become part of a two- to four-person research team and work on a project in one of the following areas: image processing, multimedia computing, neural networks, sound processing, use of the Internet, and virtual reality simulations. Although no formal education in computing is required, it is assumed that all participants will have some prior experience in computer use. *Application deadline: May 1.*

Host School:	Furman University
Type:	Computer Science and Technology
Location:	Greenville, SC
Duration:	Four weeks
Dates:	Mid-June through early July
Qualifications:	Entering grades 11 and 12. The program is designed for students interested in mathematics and science who wish to learn more about the science of computing. Admission is competitive.
Housing:	Participants are housed in the dormitories and have meals in the dining hall.
Costs:	None. Limited travel allowances, as well as need-based stipends, are offered to qualified students.
Credits Given:	None
Contact:	Dr. Kenneth Abernethy
	Young Scholars Program in Computing
	Furman University
	Department of Computer Science
	Greenville, SC 29613
	(803) 294-2097; FAX (803) 294-2058

Young Scholars Program in Engineering

The University of Kentucky's Young Scholars Program, supported through grants from the National Science Foundation, is designed to acquaint young people with the challenges and rewards to be found in engineering. Classroom activities, involving extensive use of computers, introduce students to disciplines that include agricultural, chemical, civil, electrical, mechanical, and mining engineering, as well as materials science. Students use engineering physics to solve real-world problems. Field trips to manufacturing plants and a mining operation provide participants with the opportunity to "shadow" a practicing engineer. Workshops on ethics, cooperative education, college admissions, and financial aid are also part of the program. An independent project during the school year completes the cycle. *Application deadline: April 15.*

Host School:	University of Kentucky
Type:	Engineering
Location:	Lexington, KY
Duration:	Three weeks
Dates:	Early through late June
Qualifications:	Entering grades 11 and 12. Open to high-achieving students who enjoy using mathematics and scientific principles to solve problems and who are residents of Kentucky, West Virginia, Ohio, Virginia, Indiana, or Tennessee. Chemistry and Algebra II are prerequisites.
Housing:	Participants are housed in residence halls and have meals in the dining halls.
Costs:	None
Credits Given:	None
Contact:	Charles Hamrin, Jr.
	Young Scholars Program in Engineering
	University of Kentucky
	College of Engineering
	163 Anderson Hall
	Lexington, KY 40506-0046
	(606) 257-4959; FAX (606) 323-1929

Young Scholars Program:
Introduction to Engineering and Computers Workshop

The Young Scholars Program at Tennessee Tech has been designed to provide high school students with science experiences unavailable at their home schools; the program is centered on engineering. The program's goals are to improve students' awareness of career options in engineering and to stimulate creativity and problem-solving ability. It also hopes to help students gain an understanding of the interrelationships between energy production and the environment. The program includes lectures on engineering and current concerns, computer programming (using FORTRAN 77), and engineering design. Each participant conducts a research project. Field trips and individual career and financial counseling are provided. Recreational activities are scheduled in the evenings and on some weekends. **Application deadline: May 1.**

Host School:	Tennessee Technological University
Type:	Engineering and Computers
Location:	Cookeville, TN
Duration:	Four weeks
Dates:	Mid-June through mid-July
Qualifications:	Entering grades 11 and 12. Students should rank in the top 20 percent of their class in science and mathematics.
Housing:	Participants are housed in a university dormitory and have meals at the University Center.
Costs:	$25 registration fee
Credits Given:	None
Contact:	Mr. Tony Marable
	Young Scholars Program: Introduction to Engineering and Computers
	Tennessee Technological University
	College of Engineering
	N. Peachtree Avenue
	Cookeville, TN 38505
	(615) 372-3172; FAX (615) 372-6172

Young Scholars Research Participation Program in Aquatic Ecology

Participants in the Aquatic Ecology program become members of a research team working at a field site in the Mt. Hood National Forest. The program begins at Three Lynx School, where students receive basic training in field techniques. Studies focus on the plants, animals, and ecology of the Clackamas River and its surrounding watersheds and wetlands. The group then moves to a research site on the upper Clackamas River, where participants begin four weeks of intensive field research. The relationship between forest and aquatic resource management is explored through a study of the salmon habitats in the region. The students gain hands-on experience with the high-tech equipment currently in use by the Forest Service. Included are such state-of-the-art technologies as satellite imagery, a global positioning system, and a geographic information system. *Application deadline: April 1.*

Host School:	Oregon Museum of Science and Industry (OMSI)
Type:	Ecology Field Experience
Location:	Various sites in Oregon
Duration:	Six weeks
Dates:	Early June through early August
Qualifications:	Entering grades 10 through 12. Open to students ages 15 through 18 who have a demonstrated interest in science and especially in freshwater and/or fisheries.
Housing:	Students live in A-frame cabins and eat in the dining hall while at the Hancock Field Station. Wilderness camping is a part of the field experience.
Costs:	None
Credits Given:	None
Contact:	Dr. Jeffry Gottfried
	Young Scholars Research Participation Programs in Aquatic Ecology
	Oregon Museum of Science and Industry (OMSI)
	1945 SE Water Avenue
	Portland, OR 97214
	(503) 797-4571; FAX (503) 797-4568

Young Scholars Research Participation Program in Archaeology

Budding archaeologists have a unique opportunity to live and work as field researchers during the six weeks of this OMSI Young Scholars Program. High school members of the Archaeology Research Team work under the direction and guidance of professional researchers and educators, and gain a firsthand look at the world of the professional scientist. The program begins with basic archaeological training and orientation at the historic Skyliners' Lodge near Bend, Oregon, and moves to a variety of field sites as students study the region's Native American rock art sites. Students conduct site surveys, assist in the excavation of both historic and pre-contact sites, and visit the site of the oldest shelter structure in the Western Hemisphere. Field sites include the rock art area on Tumalo Creek, work around Pine Mountain, and field work on the Crooked River National Grasslands. The program concludes in Portland, analyzing the rock art and prepraring final reports for presentation on individual research projects. **Application deadline: April 1.**

Host School:	Oregon Museum of Science and Industry (OMSI)
Type:	Archaeology Field Experience
Location:	Central Oregon
Duration:	Six weeks
Dates:	Late June through early August
Qualifications:	Entering grades 11 and 12. Students should have a demonstrated interest in science and especially in archaeology.
Housing:	Students live in A-frame cabins and eat in the dining hall while at the Hancock Field Station. Most of the time is spent in wilderness camping at the field sites.
Costs:	None
Credits Given:	None
Contact:	Dr. Jeffry Gottfried
	Young Scholars Research Participation Program in Archaeology
	Oregon Museum of Science and Industry (OMSI)
	1945 SE Water Avenue
	Portland, OR 97214
	(503) 797-4571; FAX (503) 797-4568

Young Scholars Research Participation Program in Paleontology/Geology

Participants have a unique opportunity to live the life of a paleontologist for the summer. For three weeks, students work in two field environments, collecting and studying fossil plants and animals near Hancock Station in central Oregon and from the Ochoco Mountains in eastern Oregon. After work in the field, participants return to the laboratory near Portland for analysis of fossil finds, fossil preparation, library research, and presentation of individual research projects. For the six weeks of this program, students engage in research activities under the direction of outstanding researchers, participate in numerous field trips and wilderness camping experiences, and are introduced to the world of the professional scientist while interacting with other talented high school students. *Application deadline: April 1.*

Host School:	Oregon Museum of Science and Industry (OMSI)
Type:	Paleontology and Geology Field Experience
Location:	Various sites in Oregon
Duration:	Six weeks
Dates:	Late June through early August
Qualifications:	Entering grades 11 and 12. Students should demonstrate interest in science and especially in paleontology.
Housing:	Students live in A-frame cabins and eat in the dining hall while at the Hancock Field Station. Wilderness camping is a part of the field experience.
Costs:	None
Credits Given:	None
Contact:	Dr. Jeffry Gottfried
	Young Scholars Research Participation Program in Paleontology/Geology
	Oregon Museum of Science and Industry (OMSI)
	1945 SE Water Avenue
	Portland, OR 97214
	(503) 797-4571; FAX (503) 797-4568

$\mathbb{S}$tudent $\mathbb{P}$rofile

Raina Croff
Portland, Ore.
Young Scholars Research
Participation Program in
Paleontology/Geology

Raina has been involved in summer programs since she was eleven. Her experience as a Young Scholar has led her to consider a career in archaeology.

My OMSI experience began at the age of eleven at Camp Hancock in central Oregon. This experience introduced me not only to the beautiful high desert of Oregon, but also to a whole world of science. What began as an OMSI camp experience would later mature into a serious career interest for me. At Camp Hancock, I was amazed to discover that an area which appeared so dead on the surface was actually full of life, assuming many forms, from sagebrush and juniper to wildlife and even fossils. What fascinated me was that from all these different aspects came the desert as a whole living ecosystem where even I had a part to play.

I was fortunate enough to visit Hancock Field Station again in the summer of my seventh-grade year as a counselor's aid. Once again I found myself learning still more of the world of natural science, as well as teaching younger kids.

In the summer of my sophomore year, I was accepted into the OMSI Young Scholars Program as a member of the Paleontology Research Team. Through my earlier experiences with OMSI science camps, my interest in the study of the natural past had been sparked. As an OMSI Young Scholar, I was shown the real world of scientific discovery. Days in the field were educational, enriching classrooms, bounded not by four walls, but only by the intensity of our desired to learn. Conducting hands-on experiments and actual scientific documentation, my scope of the world of science before me was broadened as my interests in careers in science gradually came into focus.

The following summer, I was asked back to be the returning Young Scholar on the Archaeology Research Team. This experience would later prove as the most valuable experience thus far in the OMSI programs, for through this program my career interest became clear; I would explore the scientific world of the past as an archaeologist.

Young Scholars Research Program in Chemistry

Participants in the Young Scholars Research Program become active members of a research team engaged in an aspect of current chemistry research. Students may choose to take part in study in one of the traditional areas such as inorganic, organic, analytical, or physical chemistry. They may also choose to participate in ongoing research in neurochemistry, biochemistry, chemical physics, geochemistry, and materials chemistry. In addition to the research participation, students take part in seminars and discussions and trips to IBM, Corning Glass, Procter & Gamble, and environmental research facilities. Weekend activities include both educational and recreational field trips. *Application deadline: April 1.*

Host School: Binghamton University, State University of New York
Type: Chemistry Research Internship
Location: Binghamton, NY
Duration: Six weeks
Dates: End of June through the first week of August
Qualifications: Entering grade 12. Applicants must be science oriented with a strong background in mathematics and must have a high school average of at least 90 percent or rank in the top 15 percent of their class.
Housing: Participants are housed in a residence hall and have meals in the dining hall.
Costs: No cost to participants. Minimal travel expenses are also provided.
Credits Given: 4 college credits
Contact: Young Scholars Research Program in Chemistry
Binghamton University, State University of New York
Department of Chemistry
P.O. Box 6000
Binghamton, NY 13902-6000
(607) 777-2208; FAX (607) 777-4478

The Young Scientist Biomedical Research Program

Florida students interested in medical research are paired with university researchers, serving as mentors and teachers to guide students in their work. Research is conducted in a variety of biomedical-related areas, including laboratory research studies in genetics, molecular biology, neuroanatomy, and biochemistry. Students utilize the university's libraries and data bases for reading and to acquire background in their field of study. Laboratory experiments are performed in their mentor's lab. The program is designed to increase student interest in science-related careers. Evening and weekend activities include recreational programs and field trips. **Contact the program director for application deadline.**

Host School:	Florida International University
Type:	Biomedical Research Internship
Location:	Miami, FL
Duration:	One month
Dates:	Early July through early August
Qualifications:	Entering grades 11 and 12. Open to Florida minority students interested in biomedical research.
Housing:	Participants are housed in dormitories and have meals in the dining halls.
Costs:	No cost to participants.
Credits Given:	One unit of elective high school credit
Contact:	Newton Moore
	The Young Scientist Biomedical Research Program
	Florida International University
	University Park
	Miami, FL 33199
	(305) 348-2436

Comprehensive Programs

Academic Enrichment for the Gifted in Summer (AEGIS)

The AEGIS programs are open to any qualified student within the state of Arkansas. Students engage in an intensive learning experience selected from a variety of academic offerings. The programs available change each summer, although some have run for a number of years. Typical of the offerings for day students are the following: Project SMILE (Studying Mathematics in Laboratory Experiments), in which students perform experiments and analyze data in the computer laboratory at Conway Middle School; PRE-MED (Providing Real Experiences in Medical Education), for students interested in careers in the medical health field; Forecasting a Better Future through Technology, in which students focus on the uses of technology while developing computer skills; Laureate International Studies (LIS), for an understanding of international issues; a Summer Chemistry Institute at the University of Arkansas, Little Rock; and a Summer Science Institute at the National Center for Toxicological Research in Pine Bluff, in which students work with professional researchers. *Interested students should contact the program administrator for information about the upcoming summer offerings and application information.*

Host School:	Various schools throughout Arkansas
Type:	Selected subjects
Location:	Various sites throughout Arkansas
Duration:	Two to three weeks
Dates:	Selected weeks in June and July
Qualifications:	Entering grades 7 through 12. AEGIS programs are open to motivated Arkansas students interested in summer enrichment activities in a variety of program areas.
Housing:	The programs listed are day programs. No housing is provided. AEGIS also offers a number of residential programs described in other listings.
Costs:	None
Credits Given:	None
Contact:	Ann Biggers
	Academic Enrichment for the Gifted in Summer (AEGIS)
	Arkansas Department of Education
	4 State Capitol Mall
	Little Rock, AR 72201-1071
	(501) 682-4224

Advance College Experience (ACE)

Jointly sponsored by Ripon College and Parents and Children for Excellence (PACE), the Advance College Experience (ACE) program provides upper elementary through high school students with an opportunity to take academic enrichment classes in a college setting. Students choose from a wide variety of classes, generally taking two courses during this special summer session. Subjects offered include: basic programming, chemistry, creative writing, drawing and painting, physics, Spanish, insect biology, journalism, mathematics, signing for the deaf, storytelling, songwriting, theater, and watercolor. Some classes are open to students and an adult co-learner, so that student and parent might share the summer learning experience. Students who have previously participated in the ACE program might opt to become "Assistant College Educators" and work in a classroom under the direction of a master teacher. ***Application deadline: April 7. After this date, classes are filled on a space-available basis.***

Host School:	Ripon College
Type:	Summer Enrichment Classes
Location:	Ripon, WI
Duration:	Two weeks
Dates:	Middle to late July
Qualifications:	Entering grades 4 through 12. Open to motivated students of above-average academic ability.
Housing:	Accommodations are available in the Ripon area, but this is generally a commuter program.
Costs:	$100 for one course, $175 for two courses. Student assistants receive free tuition. Fees include instructional costs, materials, and snacks. A limited number of need-based scholarships are available.
Credits Given:	None
Contact:	Advance College Experience (ACE)
	Ripon College
	300 Seward Street
	P.O. Box 248
	Ripon, WI 54971
	(414) 748-8326

Arkansas Governor's School

The Arkansas Governor's School challenges students to expand their conceptual abilities, to develop their own theories, and discuss issues within the fields of the arts and sciences. Using what they've learned, the students integrate their acquired knowledge with modern society's views of the world. Participants take aptitude development classes in one of eight specialized fields: choral music, drama, English/language arts, instrumental music, mathematics, natural science, social science or visual arts. In addition to their specialized subjects, all students attend general classes in conceptual development and in personal and social growth. Guest speakers, concerts, films, and dramatic productions all provide experiences to enhance and enrich the classroom curriculum. ***Contact the program or high school guidance counselor for application information.***

Host School:	Hendrix College
Type:	Comprehensive
Location:	Conway, AR
Duration:	Six weeks
Dates:	Mid-June through late July
Qualifications:	Entering grade 12. Open to gifted and talented Arkansas residents. Students are nominated by their high schools; selection is competitive.
Housing:	Participants are housed and have meals on campus.
Costs:	None
Credits Given:	None
Contact:	Ann Biggers
	Arkansas Governor's School
	Hendrix College
	Department of Education
	4 State Capitol Mall
	Little Rock, AR 72201-1071
	(501) 682-4224

Backcountry Volunteers Program

The Backcountry Volunteers Program provides participants with an opportunity to give something back to the land for the enjoyment they have received from it. Volunteers work on a variety of projects located in state and national parks and forests. In past summers, work has included building trails in Alaska, weeding out nonnative plants in Hawaii, and assisting in the building of a suspension bridge at Yellowstone National Park. Most work projects take place in remote areas with the volunteer team partnered with supervisory personnel. They hike into the region, taking time to enjoy their spectacular surroundings. The work is physically demanding but extremely rewarding. Participants join teams of 10 to 12 people, ranging in age from 13 to 70. Each team works 10 days of a two-week period. Time is provided for relaxation and backcountry trips. Spring and fall trips may also be arranged. *Contact the program for information about upcoming volunteer vacation opportunities.*

Host School:	Backcountry Volunteers
Type:	Volunteer Service
Location:	Selected sites across the country
Duration:	Two weeks
Dates:	Various dates throughout the summer
Qualifications:	At least 16 years of age. (Student volunteers under 16 may attend if accompanied by a parent or guardian.) Volunteers need to be in good physical condition with the ability to walk 5 to 10 miles per day, and able to live outdoors and do hard manual labor.
Housing:	Participants supply their own camping equipment. Food is provided by the host agencies.
Costs:	$40 registration fee. Volunteers are expected to pay for their own transportation to and from worksite.
Credits Given:	None
Contact:	Backcountry Volunteers Program
	Backcountry Volunteers
	P.O. Box 86
	North Scituate, MA 02060-0086
	(617) 545-7019

Breckenridge Outdoor Education Center Internships

Here's a program where the individual can truly make a difference! The Breckenridge Outdoor Education Center provides year-round, adventure-based wilderness programs for people with disabilities. The program focuses on empowering its participants to experience both physical and emotional success, as they realize their full potential. The instructional staff, assisted by volunteer interns, are committed to these goals. Programs at the center change by season and clientele, but have included sit and mono skiing, high-ropes courses, backpacking, snowshoeing, rock climbing, cross-country skiing, and environmental awareness activities. Groups have included cancer patients, spinal cord and head injury patients, the hearing impaired, the developmentally disabled, and people with multiple disabilities. Interns work with the center's professional staff, teaching disabled people to enjoy the outdoors. *Application deadline: March for the summer session.*

Host School:	Breckenridge Outdoor Education Center (BOEC)
Type:	Internship
Location:	Breckenridge, CO
Duration:	Three months
Dates:	Late May to the end of August
Qualifications:	Interns must be at least high school graduates. A background in wilderness skills and/or a desire to work with the handicapped are needed, as well as enthusiasm, interest in learning, and willingness to contribute.
Housing:	Housing and meals are provided at the center.
Costs:	None
Credits Given:	None
Contact:	Breckenridge Outdoor Education Center Internships
	Breckenridge Outdoor Education Center (BOEC)
	P.O. Box 697
	Breckenridge, CO 80424
	(303) 453-6422

Communications Arts, Sciences, and Technology in Harmony: Technoculture

This Michigan Summer Institute focuses on the performing and communications arts, the social sciences, and communication technologies to examine the importance and impact of communication in our world. Students choose an area for intensive study from offerings that include both arts and sciences. The intensive arts courses include: music as a universal language, acting, problem solving through the arts, and multimedia design, production, and control. Science intensives study artificial life (robotics), physics of light and sound, and technology and culture in the urban environment. Students may also choose to concentrate in the law, the psychology of communication, leadership styles, or in intercultural communication. All classes involve class discussions, guest speakers, field trips, and activities. Evening peer-group discussions tackle any topic of interest to the group, while a wide range of recreational activities round out this dynamic program. *Application deadline: February 28.*

Host School:	Eastern Michigan University
Type:	Communications
Location:	Ypsilanti, MI
Duration:	Two weeks
Dates:	Late June through mid-July
Qualifications:	Entering grades 11 and 12. Open to current Michigan public and private school students.
Housing:	Participants are housed in dormitories and have meals in the dining hall.
Costs:	$200. Local and state need-based scholarships are available.
Credits Given:	None
Contact:	Dave Gore
	Communications Arts, Sciences, and Technology in Harmony: Technoculture
	Eastern Michigan University
	Michigan Summer Institute
	Ypsilanti, MI 48197
	(313) 487-1161

Creative Connections Institute

Creative Connections, offered by the Ohio Institute for Gifted and Talented Students, seeks to challenge students interested in a more intensive learning experience. Participants choose a major course of study and an afternoon elective. The morning sessions focus on hands-on experiences and creative problem solving, incorporating the completion of an individual or group project. Classes offered change each year, but the following are representative of courses available: the Secrets of Higher Math, Using your "Write" Brain, Great Words and Greater Ideas, Careers in Medicine and Health Care, Biology Busters, and Archaeology. Afternoon electives have a lighter flavor such as Afternoon at the Improv, Computer Assisted Design, Math Magic, Newspaper Production, and Shakespeare. Evening activities include special programs and activities such as guest lectures and simulation games. *Application deadline: early April.*

Host School:	Kent State University
Type:	Selected subjects
Location:	Kent, OH
Duration:	One week
Dates:	Four sessions held during July
Qualifications:	Entering grades 10 and 11. Open to Ohio students recognized by their school district as gifted or talented and interested in advanced learning in any of the Creative Connections course offerings.
Housing:	Participants are housed in residence halls and have meals in the dining hall.
Costs:	$180
Credits Given:	None
Contact:	Creative Connections Institute
	Kent State University
	College of Continuing Studies
	P.O. Box 5190
	Kent, OH 44242-0001
	(216) 672-3102

The Center for Talented Youth (CTY) Challenge Awards Program

Each year a select group of students highly talented in the arts and the humanities receive the opportunity to take part in scientific research at field stations across North America. The purpose of this program is to inspire creative students to expand their fields of interest to include science. In the past few years, students have engaged in research on a variety of topics at stations that have included the Woods Hole Oceanographic Institute in Massachusetts, the Institute of Northern Forestry in Alaska, and NASA's Jet Propulsion Laboratory in California. Students are assigned in small teams of 7 to 10 students and work alongside outstanding researchers. A graduate student assistant and a resident adviser also assist and are housed with the students. Participants keep a personal journal and gain an understanding of the importance of science in everyday life. ***Nomination deadline: December 15. Application deadline: January 25.***

Host School:	Johns Hopkins University Center for Talented Youth (CTY)
Type:	Scientific Field Research
Location:	At various sites throughout the nation.
Duration:	Two weeks
Dates:	Various dates between late June and mid-August
Qualifications:	Entering grades 11, 12, and precollege freshmen at least 16 years of age. Students should demonstrate considerable ability in the arts and the humanities, demonstrate an interest in the natural world, and be nominated by their schools.
Housing:	Students are housed on site at the assigned research station. Meals are provided.
Costs:	No cost to participants. All travel and field costs are provided.
Credits Given:	None
Contact:	The CTY Challenge Awards Program
	Johns Hopkins University Center for Talented Youth (CTY)
	3400 North Charles Street
	Baltimore, MD 21218-2699
	(410) 516-0337

$\mathbb{F}$lorida Governor's Summer Programs

The Florida Governor's Program sponsors a variety of educational enrichment programs each summer across the state. Although some programs are residential, most are day programs that serve students from the surrounding areas. The programs are offered in a wide range of interest areas. Past offerings have included such programs as law studies through the Criminal Law and Social Values program at Florida State University; a six-week marine/wetland resource management program, the Ecology of St. Andrew's Bay, at Gulf Coast Community College; a math, computer, and science program at Hillsborough Community College; a visual anthropology and environmental education program entitled An Interdisciplinary Approach to the People and Environment of North Florida at Lake City Community College; an Afro-Caribbean Dance History Practicum at Santa Fe Community College; a documentary filmmaking program at Seminole Community College; and an environmental issues program, "Florida, Saving Its Story," at Valencia Community College. *Contact your guidance counselor or gifted coordinator or the Governor's Program office for upcoming offerings and application information and deadlines.*

Host School:	Florida State University System
Type:	Selected Subjects
Location:	Various sites around the state
Duration:	Two to six weeks
Dates:	Summer
Qualifications:	Entering grades 8 through 12. Open to gifted and high-ability Florida students interested in offerings provided. Each program has its own focus and target group of students.
Housing:	Day programs. No housing is provided.
Costs:	None
Credits Given:	Many of the programs provide for elective high school credits.
Contact:	Florida Governor's Summer Programs
	Florida State University System
	Florida Department of Education
	Division of Public Schools—Bureau of Education for Exceptional Students
	Tallahassee, FL
	(904) 488-1106; FAX (904) 922-7088

Georgia Governor's Honors Program

The Georgia Governor's Honors Program is designed to provide a summer of challenging and enriching activities to gifted students. The program seeks to give participants opportunities to acquire the skills needed to become independent, lifelong learners. Each student takes part in an intensive study in an academic or artistic field of their choice. Courses are available in English, foreign languages, mathematics, science and social studies, as well as in art, theater, music, dance, design, technology, and executive management. Students also select a minor area for study, choosing from selections similar to those available for intensive study. In addition to these courses, instruction is also provided in four support areas—computers, counseling, library/media, and physical fitness. Performing groups including orchestra, band, chorus, and theater companies attract students from all major areas of study. Seminars, special events, sports, and planned recreational programs complete this program. *Contact program director for application deadline.*

Host School:	Valdosta State University
Type:	Comprehensive
Location:	Valdosta, GA
Duration:	Six weeks
Dates:	Late June through early August
Qualifications:	Entering grades 11 and 12. Open to intellectually gifted and artistically talented students currently enrolled in Georgia's public and private high schools and nominated by their teachers.
Housing:	Participants are housed in dormitories and have meals in the dining halls.
Costs:	None
Credits Given:	None
Contact:	Georgia Governor's Honors Program
	Valdosta State University
	Georgia Department of Education
	2054 Twin Towers East, Capitol Square
	Atlanta, GA 30334-5040
	(404) 656-5812

The Governor's School of North Carolina

Each summer eight hundred gifted and talented North Carolina students spend six weeks in an intensive summer program at one of two Governor's Schools. The students take classes in three areas. Area I subjects meet twice a day and focus on contemporary issues and ideas of the twentieth century. Area I students must be selected for the program and choose from classes that include art, choral music, dance, drama, English, foreign language (French and Spanish), instrumental music, mathematics, natural science, and social science. Students also take part in Area II classes—a study of the nature of philosophy with an emphasis on twentieth-century thought. Area III classes involve a study of self in society, courses that encourage self-exploration and self-discovery. Area II and III classes include students from both academic and fine arts specializations. Recreational and social programs complement the program. ***Application deadline: early January.***

Host School:	Governor's School East: St. Andrews Presbyterian College
	Governor's School West: Salem College
Type:	Comprehensive
Location:	East: Laurinburg, NC
	West: Winston-Salem, NC
Duration:	Six weeks
Dates:	Late June through early August
Qualifications:	Entering grade 12 for all areas except for the visual/performing arts, which also accepts students in grade 11. Open to academically gifted North Carolina residents nominated by their schools.
Housing:	Participants are housed in dormitories and have meals in the dining facilities.
Costs:	No cost to participants.
Credits Given:	None
Contact:	Special Assistant
	The Governor's School of North Carolina
	Exceptional Children Support Team
	North Carolina Department of Public Instruction
	301 N. Wilmington Street
	Raleigh, NC 27601-2825
	(919) 715-1994

Habitat for Humanity Project

Habitat for Humanity, a nonprofit, ecumenical Christian housing ministry, works in partnership with individuals and groups to build houses with and for families who would be otherwise unable to afford decent shelter. Habitat volunteers, both skilled and unskilled, work together with the prospective homeowners to construct houses and thus help to eliminate poverty housing. Local Habitat affiliates sponsor work camps for groups and individuals during busy building times. Students can get experience in construction during a work camp, working alongside skilled volunteers. Benefits of a work camp experience include the satisfaction derived through service to others, the sense of fellowship that comes from living with and working closely with a diverse group of individuals, and the pride that follows the successful building of a home. ***Contact the program's Help Line at (912) 924-6935, ext. 551 or 552, for the location of your nearest affiliate.***

Host School:	Habitat for Humanity International
Type:	Volunteer Program
Location:	Various sites across the United States and abroad
Duration:	One to three weeks
Dates:	Throughout the summer and school year
Qualifications:	Over 18 for most projects, although students 16 and over are welcome at many work camp projects across the United States and Canada.
Housing:	Work camps provide housing and food for volunteers.
Costs:	Volunteers pay for their own transportation to and from the worksite.
Credits Given:	None
Contact:	Habitat for Humanity Project
	Habitat for Humanity International
	121 Habitat Street
	Americus, GA 31709-3498
	(912) 924-6935; FAX (912) 924-6541

Intern '96

Thirty rising high school seniors are invited to participate in a unique opportunity with the Smithsonian Internship program each summer, exploring possible career options while they explore the Smithsonian and Washington, D.C. Each intern spends about 35 hours per week working in a specific office with a Smithsonian professional. Students apply for one of the openings listed in the application booklet. Positions include varied opportunities, such as the chance to assist the communications staff of the Friends of the National Zoo, to work in lighting design or with computers at the National Air and Space Museum, to intern in the Curator's Office at the National Museum of American Art, to assist veterinary technicians at the National Zoological Park, or to help the director of the Discovery Theater of Smithsonian Associates. Interns may build exhibits, mount birds, maintain collections, assist in planning activities, research artists, or perform a variety of other tasks. The entire group of interns tour sites that many visitors to Washington never see. *Application deadline: March 12.*

Host School:	Smithsonian Institution
Type:	Internship
Location:	Washington, D.C.
Duration:	Six weeks
Dates:	Late June through early August
Qualifications:	Entering grade 12. Acceptance is based on a demonstrated interest in a particular subject area or career. Minority students and students with disabilities are especially encouraged to apply.
Housing:	Participants are housed in a residence hall. Meals are the responsibility of the interns.
Costs:	None. Each intern earns an allowance of $700 to cover meals and living expenses. Round-trip travel tickets are provided for students living outside of the Washington, D.C., area.
Credits Given:	None
Contact:	Intern '96
	Smithsonian Institution
	Office of Elementary and Secondary Education
	A & I, Room 1163, MRC 402
	Washington, DC 20560
	(202) 357-3049

International Workcamps

International Workcamps are an inexpensive and meaningful way in which individuals can travel, live, and work in a foreign country. They also serve as short-term "peace corps," incorporating members from around the world. This is an excellent way for students to really get to know other people, by working and living with them and improving their lives in a tangible way. Workcamps are sponsored by an organization in the host country, but are coordinated by people in the local community that they serve. Generally, they are comprised of 10 to 20 people from four or more countries. Participants are housed in facilities that range from schools, churches, private homes, and community centers to campgrounds. Workcampers engage in communal living, sharing food preparation, work projects, and recreation. Most workcamp projects involve construction, restoration, and agricultural, social, or environmental work. During free time, Workcampers are involved in local excursions, discussions, and recreational activities. To participate, register on a first-come, first-served basis beginning in early April. **VFP's directory ($12) lists over 800 workcamps around the world.**

Host School:	Volunteers for Peace (VFP), Inc.
Type:	Volunteer Service
Location:	Workcamps are held around the world in 60 countries
Duration:	Two to three weeks
Dates:	Throughout the summer and during the school year
Qualifications:	Age 16 and up. Many workcamps have a minimum age of 18, although younger students are welcome in camps in Russia, France, and Germany.
Housing:	Volunteers are housed at or near the site of the work projects selected. Living conditions are generally Spartan and may include tents or communal accommodations. Volunteers are generally asked to bring a sleeping bag. All meals are provided by the workcamp's sponsors.
Costs:	$150 registration fee.
Credits Given:	None
Contact:	International Workcamps
	Volunteers for Peace (VFP), Inc.
	43 Tiffany Road
	Belmont, VT 05730
	(802) 259-2759; FAX (802) 259-2922

Kansas Regents Honors Academy

In a program hosted by a different Kansas university each year, the Kansas Board of Regents offers academically gifted Kansas students the opportunity to participate in this challenging summer experience. Students choose one specially designed class in addition to a core course. The core selection, Critical Texts and Concepts, provides an intensive introduction to the humanities, examining concepts influential in civilization development. Further study into the implications and possible consequences of these values in our time and in the future are also explored. Additional courses presented in recent summers have included War and Society in America, Discovering the Environment, Mass Media, and Work, Economics, and the Arts. Supplementary cultural and social events, including art exhibits, films, theater, dances, picnics, and tours, provide enriching experiences. Lectures by eminent guest speakers and personal development workshops, as well as a full program of recreational and sports activities, complete this exciting summer program. ***Application deadline: Contact program coordinator for information.***

Host School:	Kansas State University
Type:	Comprehensive
Location:	Manhattan, KS
Duration:	Four weeks
Dates:	July
Qualifications:	Entering grades 11 and 12. Open to outstanding Kansas students, chosen on a competitive basis.
Housing:	Participants are housed in dormitories and have meals in the dining halls.
Costs:	No cost to participants.
Credits Given:	College credits are available at additional cost.
Contact:	Dr. Judith Zivanovic
	Kansas Regents Honors Academy
	Kansas State University
	Honors Program, College of Arts and Sciences
	116 Eisenhower Hall
	Manhattan, KS 66506-1005
	(913) 532-6902

Kentucky Governor's Scholars Program

Designed to motivate and empower Kentucky's brightest young people to become contributing citizens, the Governor's Scholars Program seeks to broaden the horizons of its 700 participants. Through nontraditional courses and independent learning, students are encouraged to develop their conceptual and critical thinking skills. The curriculum features an in-depth experience in a focus area that includes astronomy, biological issues, cultural anthropology, fine arts, historical analyses, language and culture (French, Japanese, Russian, or Spanish), literary studies, modes of mathematical thinking, philosophy, physical science, and social, political, and economic theory. Problem-solving studies emphasize inquiry, research, and solution development. The Governor's Scholars Program focuses on personal growth, exploring such topics as interpersonal communications, college choices, civic responsibility, and relationships. Scholars plan for personal involvement in service projects for their schools or communities; projects are implemented when students return to their homes. Planned evening and weekend activities and visits from noted scientists, writers, and community leaders complete this stimulating summer experience. Schools nominate students to become part of this program. *Application deadline: January 31.*

Host School:	Centre College and Northern Kentucky University
Type:	Selected Subjects
Location:	Danville, KY, and Highland Heights, KY
Duration:	Five weeks
Dates:	Late June through late July
Qualifications:	Entering grade 12. Open to Kentucky residents who are enrolled in a public or private high school in Kentucky. High PSAT, SAT, or ACT scores or special talents are required. Competitive admissions.
Housing:	Participants are housed in dormitories and have meals in the dining halls.
Costs:	No cost to participants.
Credits Given:	None
Contact:	Kentucky Governor's Scholars Program
	Centre College and Northern Kentucky University
	Office of the Governor
	Frankfort, KY 40601
	(502) 564-3553

Martin W. Essex School for the Gifted

Each summer, some of Ohio's most able young people come together for an intensive and challenging weeklong experience exploring complex and abstract ideas, encouraging them to become leaders and contributors to society. Activities for the week include classes, seminars, workshops, and independent study in a variety of subjects. Student studies include government, science, the arts, the environment, global education, human resources, future studies, and career planning. Students explore the Internet, participate in a panel discussion with government officials, take part in team building and challenge initiatives, and attend special-interest workshops. Group projects, such as development of an institute newspaper, encourage interaction among students and peers. Field trips, recreational activities, and opportunities to create and explore academic and artistic pursuits at a level beyond that possible in the students' home schools add to this enriching week. Through this program, the students have an opportunity to experience the joys and responsibilities associated with being "gifted." ***Contact program coordinator for application information.***

Host School:	Ohio State University
Type:	Comprehensive
Location:	Columbus, OH
Duration:	One week
Dates:	Beginning of August
Qualifications:	Entering grade 12. Open to exceptional students from each school district in Ohio who have been nominated by their schools for this program.
Housing:	Participants are housed in residence halls and have meals in campus dining facilities and Columbus restaurants.
Costs:	None
Credits Given:	None
Contact:	John Herner
	Martin W. Essex School for the Gifted
	Department of Education, Division of Special Education
	933 High Street
	Worthington, OH 43085-4087
	(614) 466-2650

Maryland Summer Centers for Gifted and Talented Students

The Maryland Summer Centers Partnership Network offers the state's gifted and talented students a selection of interesting academic enrichment courses each summer. Students choose a class offered in their desired field and apply directly to the program coordinator for the individual course. Typical offerings include: Civil War Studies at Prince George's Community College, an interdisciplinary approach to the Civil War; archaeology at the Oregon Ridge Nature Center and at St. Mary's College, an investigation of past cultures through field and labwork; Math and Technology at the University of Maryland's Eastern Shore; and arts programs at Salisbury State University and Goucher College. Programs offered may change each summer. Some offerings are open to both Maryland and out-of-state students. ***Please contact program coordinator for current selections and application deadlines.***

Host School:	Maryland State Department of Education
Type:	Selected Subjects
Location:	Various sites around Maryland
Duration:	One to three weeks
Dates:	Late June through mid-August
Qualifications:	Entering grades 4 through 12. Open to all Maryland residents.
Housing:	The programs include a mixture of residential and commuter offerings.
Costs:	Tuition ranges from $100 to $425, with most programs in the lower portion of the range. Need-based financial aid is available.
Credits Given:	None
Contact:	Dr. Judith Stough
	Maryland Summer Centers for Gifted and Talented Students
	Maryland State Department of Education
	Arts and Sciences Branch
	200 West Baltimore Street
	Baltimore, MD 21201
	(410) 767-0362; FAX (410)333-2379

Michigan Summer Institute: The Art of Science and the Science of Art

The program's theme is the Art of Science and the Science of Art. Students are asked to explore the ways in which art and science are related by choosing an area of intensive study. Students can select from topics that include biomedical technology, chemistry, digital electronics, math, photography, storytelling, musical theater, and ceramics. The facilities of the university, the Kalamazoo Area Math and Science Center, and the Kalamazoo Institute of Art are available to participants as they engage in discussions, lab activities, field research, and attend speaker presentations. Field trips include a concert, a live theater performance, and a day at Lake Michigan. Peer group discussions consider topics critical to the lives of the participants. Sports and social activities complement the program. *Application deadline: February 28.*

Host School:	Western Michigan University
Type:	Science
Location:	Kalamazoo, MI
Duration:	Two weeks
Dates:	Middle to late July
Qualifications:	Entering grades 11 and 12. Open to current Michigan public and private school students interested in exploring the relationships between art and science.
Housing:	Participants are housed in dormitories and have meals in the dining hall.
Costs:	$200 program fee. Local and state need-based scholarships are available.
Credits Given:	None
Contact:	Diane Henderson
	Michigan Summer Institute
	Western Michigan University
	Office of Conferences and Institutes
	Kalamazoo, MI 49008
	(616) 387-4174; FAX (616) 387-4189

Michigan Summer Institute: Changing Worlds/Changing Selves

Working on the assumption that "the only constant in life is change," Madonna University presents students with a series of enrichment courses, all of which focus on the forces and agents of change in today's society. The institute is designed to develop participants' self-awareness, self-expression, and self-confidence, preparing them to meet the challenges of a changing world. Taking a futuristic approach, students attempt to identify trends and forecast what the future will be like over the next 100 years. Students choose an intensive area of study from offerings in both the arts and sciences. Arts and communication intensives include printmaking old and new, music video production, architecture (from traditional to high-tech), journalism, sign language and artistic interpretation for the deaf, and Japanese language and culture. Science-related intensives include molecular genetics and genetic engineering, garbology (studying consumption and waste), and ecology. All intensives include class discussions, field trips, and guest speakers. Evening peer-group discussions focus on topics of interest to the students. Recreational, social, and cultural activities complete the program. *Application deadline: February 28.*

Host School:	Madonna University
Type:	Arts and Sciences
Location:	Livonia, MI
Duration:	Two weeks
Dates:	Mid-July
Qualifications:	Entering grades 10 and 11. Open to Michigan residents interested in a challenging summer experience.
Housing:	Participants are housed in dormitories and have meals in the dining facilities.
Costs:	$200. Financial aid is available.
Credits Given:	None
Contact:	Sister Nancy Marie Jamroz
	Michigan Summer Institute
	Madonna University
	36600 Schoolcraft Road
	Livonia, MI 48150
	(313) 591-5055

Michigan Summer Institute at Olivet: Critical Issues and Creative Expressions for the '90s and Beyond

Olivet College offers strong critical thinkers and/or creatively expressive students a chance to go beyond traditional lecture-oriented education and experience creative, reasoning-based learning. Students involved in both academic and performance areas and those who have begun to see the connections between the arts and sciences benefit from this institute. Students choose an intensive area for study, selecting from courses that include poetry and fiction writing, jazz studies, acting, visual arts, storytelling, critical issues in American society, psychology and personality, education, and critical environmental issues. In addition to the intensive courses, students take part in a wide range of programs designed to show the interdisciplinary relationships between the creative arts and the social sciences. These relationships are explored with guest speakers, panel discussions, films, and small-group sessions. Peer-group discussions consider hot topics of interest to the institute members. Recreational and social activities and field trips complete the program. *Application deadline: February 28.*

Host School:	Olivet College
Type:	Selected Subjects
Location:	Olivet, MI
Duration:	Two weeks
Dates:	Late June through early July
Qualifications:	Entering grades 11 and 12. Open to Michigan residents seeking an intellectually and creatively challenging summer experience.
Housing:	Participants are housed in residence halls and have meals in the dining facilities.
Costs:	$200. Need-based financial aid is available.
Credits Given:	None
Contact:	Jim Donohue
	Michigan Summer Institute at Olivet
	Olivet College
	Department of Performing Arts
	Olivet, MI 49076
	(616) 749-7694

Michigan Summer Institute: Environment and Technology in the Twenty-first Century

Michigan Tech's Summer Institute investigates the current technological and environmental issues affecting students and their communities. Critical social issues are used to generate exciting problem-solving and laboratory experiences. Through a mix of formal and informal discussions, individual research, field trips, group meetings, and special presentations, students pursue studies in their chosen subject. Students may select from discipline areas that include chemistry, physics, engineering design, German language and culture, creative writing (fiction, poetry, and nonfiction), and exploring cultures through pottery and sketching. Afternoon exploratories, evening presentations, and workshops present students with opportunities to explore new ideas and fields. A full range of recreational and social activities completes this stimulating program. *Application deadline: February 28.*

Host School:	Michigan Technological University
Type:	Comprehensive
Location:	Houghton, MI
Duration:	Two weeks
Dates:	Mid-June through early July
Qualifications:	Entering grades 11 and 12. Open to current Michigan public and private school students.
Housing:	Participants are housed in residence halls and have meals in the dining hall.
Costs:	$200. Local and state need-based financial aid is available.
Credits Given:	None
Contact:	Chris Anderson
	Michigan Summer Institute
	Michigan Technological University
	1400 Townsend Drive
	Houghton, MI 49931
	(906) 487-2920; FAX (906) 487-2468

Michigan Summer Institute: Technology and the Environment/Community and Industrial Planning

Participants employ their creativity to plan possible uses for 5,200 acres of nearby land to maximize the economic and environmental needs of the region. Students work closely with professional and community leaders and regulatory agencies to seek industrial, recreational, governmental, and future uses for this area. Participants focus on environmental issues, data collection and analysis, creation of a planning document, presentation strategies, and Total Quality Management techniques (team building, brainstorming, and consensus decision making). Students also explore career opportunities including environmental engineering, community and industrial planning, air- and water-quality technology, technical writing, geography, and manufacturing resource planning. A wide range of recreational and social events rounds out the program. Contact Thomas Meravi at (906) 227-2552 or Chris Kitzman at the address below for more information. *Application deadline: February 28.*

Host School: Northern Michigan University
Type: Environmental Science and Land-Use Management
Location: Marquette, MI
Duration: One week
Dates: Mid-July
Qualifications: Entering grades 11 and 12. Open to Michigan residents interested in land use management and community planning.
Housing: Participants are housed in dormitories and have meals in the dining hall.
Costs: $200. Financial aid is available.
Credits Given: None
Contact: Chris Kitzman
Michigan Summer Institute: Technology
Ingham Intermediate School District
2630 West Howell Road
Mason, MI 48854
(517) 676-2550

The Mississippi Governor's School

This program is designed to provide academic, creative, and leadership experiences to Mississippi's outstanding students. Classes, seminars, and workshops are offered in a variety of subject areas drawn from the humanities, the fine and performing arts, philosophy, the social sciences, mathematics, and the sciences. Students take part in an intensive study of an area of their choice, learning current theory and participating in extensive work or field experiences. A major feature of this Governor's School program is a series of seminars that deal with major global issues and offer creative and practical experiences. Personal development seminars generate hot topics and raise serious questions for all participants. Students also are encouraged to consider college and career options. A wide variety of enrichment activities meet the cultural, social, athletic, and recreational needs of the students. Special events include a talent show, field day, and dances. ***Application deadline: February 28.***

Host School:	Mississippi University for Women
Type:	Comprehensive
Location:	Columbus, MS
Duration:	Three weeks
Dates:	Mid-June through early July
Qualifications:	Entering grades 11 and 12. Open to bright Mississippi residents interested in a challenging summer experience.
Housing:	Participants are housed in residence halls and have meals in the dining center.
Costs:	No cost to participants.
Credits Given:	Three semester hours of elective honors high school credits
Contact:	The Mississippi Governor's School
	Mississippi University for Women
	P.O. Box W-129
	Columbus, MS 39701
	(601) 329-7110, 329-7112

Missouri Scholars Academy

The Missouri Scholars Academy provides some of Missouri's most gifted students with the opportunity to enhance their academic skills, deepen their understanding of themselves and their abilities, and examine current issues while pursuing studies that differ from traditional educational programs. The curriculum is organized into three areas of study. Students choose a major course for intensive study based on their own interests, selecting from categories that include mathematics, science, social studies, and the humanities. A second academic minor is also chosen from these broad categories, providing students with additional knowledge. A third class in personal and social dynamics addresses the unique personal and social problems and responsibilities faced by academically gifted students. A full schedule of extracurricular activities including debate, journalism, art workshops, chorus, computer and photography clubs, theater, and creative writing classes complements the academic program. A recreation and sports program is also offered. Evening activities include concerts, films, lectures, social activities, and dances. ***Application deadline: February 10.***

Host School:	University of Missouri, Columbia
Type:	Comprehensive
Location:	Columbia, MO
Duration:	Three weeks
Dates:	Mid-June through early July
Qualifications:	Entering grade 11. The Academy is open to academically gifted Missouri public and private school students nominated by their schools.
Housing:	Participants are housed and have meals in the residence hall.
Costs:	None
Credits Given:	None
Contact:	Theodore Tarkow
	Missouri Scholars Academy
	University of Missouri, Columbia
	317 Lowry Hall
	Columbia, MO 65211
	(314) 882-4421

The New Jersey Governor's School on Public Issues

This Governor's School program's unique public issues curriculum has served as a model for Governor's School programs in other states. Participants learn about the problems that face all levels of our society and explore ways of finding solutions to these problems. Daily intensive courses focus on areas such as the environment, conflict resolution, community service, ethnic and cultural pluralism, future studies, and ethics and public policy. Topics are addressed in the context of New Jersey, but students also examine the issues from a local, national, and global standpoint. Integrative seminars allow students to see the connections between public issues and their own experiences and feelings. Daily debates, panels, simulations, films, and workshops look at a range of issues facing the public. Voluntary performing arts, community service projects, recreational activities, and study fill afternoon hours. Field trips and planned recreational and social events complete the program. **Application deadline: January 4.**

Host School:	Monmouth University
Type:	Public Issues
Location:	West Long Branch, NJ
Duration:	Four weeks
Dates:	July
Qualifications:	Entering grade 12. The program is directed to gifted and talented New Jersey students interested in learning about the problems that face their communities, state, and nation so they can be part of the solution.
Housing:	Participants are housed in dormitories and have meals in the dining facilities.
Costs:	No cost to participants.
Credits Given:	None
Contact:	Cheryl Keen
	The New Jersey Governor's School on Public Issues
	Monmouth University
	West Long Branch, NJ 07764
	(908) 571-3496; FAX (908) 571-7556

Ohio Governor's Summer Institute for the Gifted and Talented

This comprehensive institute seeks to challenge students through exploratory sessions, encouraging students to grow in their understanding of themselves, their peers, and their environment. Classes meet from 9 A.M. to 4 P.M. each day. Students choose their area of specialization from a variety of courses offered during each session. Students interested in science and technology may choose the engineering program, which includes work in computer-assisted design, robotics, computer programming, and engineering technologies. Or students might wish to specialize in biomedical sciences (studying health careers), aviation (ground school requirements), or math. Students involved in the humanities might opt for classes in theater, participating as a cast member or theater technician, or choose a class in photo design (including photography and darkroom techniques). Writing workshops are also available. Students have access to the university's recreational facilities during free time. *Application deadline: early April*.

Host School:	Shawnee State University
Type:	Comprehensive
Location:	Portsmouth, OH
Duration:	One week
Dates:	Three sessions are held from mid-July through early August
Qualifications:	Entering grades 10 and 11. Open to Ohio residents interested in a challenging summer experience.
Housing:	Participants are housed in dormitory apartments. Commuter students are also welcome.
Costs:	$10 processing fee. Residential students pay about $130 for housing; meals are available at extra cost.
Credits Given:	None
Contact:	Ohio Governor's Summer Institute for the Gifted and Talented
	Shawnee State University
	940 Second Street
	Portsmouth, OH 45662
	(614) 355-2412; FAX (614) 355-2598

Ohio Governor's Summer Institute for the Gifted and Talented—Wright State

Wright State's Summer Institute exposes participants to creative problem solving using methods applicable to the fine arts, technology, and the sciences. Classes and workshops are offered in science, math, communication, creative writing, and social issues. Working in small groups, students attempt to find solutions to selected problems by tapping into their own creative learning process and interacting with other participants. Because these students are potential leaders, discoverers, and creators, special sessions focusing on personal-social dynamics occur daily. These discussion topics include leadership, stress management, decision making, self-esteem, group dynamics, and understanding diversity and cultural differences. This part of the program seeks to aid in the development of the whole individual while promoting group interaction, cooperation, and friendship. Campus recreational and sports facilities, as well as nature trails, a biological preserve, and bookstores and libraries, are accessible to the students. *Application deadline: April 11.*

Host School:	Wright State University
Type:	Comprehensive
Location:	Dayton, OH
Duration:	One week
Dates:	Three sessions are held during the period from late June through late July
Qualifications:	Entering grades 10 and 11. Open to gifted and talented Ohio residents.
Housing:	Participants are housed in residence halls and have meals in the dining hall.
Costs:	$150.
Credits Given:	None
Contact:	Ohio Governor's Summer Institute for the Gifted and Talented
	Wright State University
	Office of Precollege Programs
	163 Millett Hall
	Dayton, OH 45435
	(513) 873-3135; FAX (513) 873-4883

Ohio Governor's Summer Institute for the Gifted and Talented—Wilmington College

Wilmington's Summer Institute offers three very different enrichment programs to appeal to the interests of Ohio's gifted students. One session explores the world of sports medicine and is appropriate for students considering careers in this field. Participants explore a variety of topics through seminars by featured professionals and extensive hands-on laboratory sessions. While learning about careers in physical therapy, orthopedics, podiatry, rehabilitation, and athletic training, students work with the same campus equipment used by the Cincinnati Bengals during their yearly summer camp. Students interested in biotechnology, veterinary medicine, animal science, and biology will enjoy the Institute's agriculture-related session. Through a combination of lectures and laboratory activities, students learn about such topics as artificial insemination, embryo transfer, parasite identification, vaccination practices, and feed analysis. Budding lawyers might opt for the law institute, utilizing the case study methods typically used in law schools and providing students with an understanding of the field of law and legal education. A mock trial highlights the session. Career advisement includes information about courses of study, study skills, and applying to college and law school. Preparation for the LSAT is an additional part of this session. Recreational activities include movies, picnics, bowling, and dances to occupy evening time. *Application deadline: April 11.*

Host School:	Wilmington College
Type:	Sports Medicine, Agriculture, and Law
Location:	Wilmington, OH
Duration:	One week
Dates:	Three sessions are held from late June through early July
Qualifications:	Entering grades 10 and 11. Open to Ohio residents who are eligible for gifted and talented programs.
Housing:	Participants are housed in dormitories and have meals in the dining facilities.
Costs:	$95.
Credits Given:	None
Contact:	Dr. James Boland
	Ohio Governor's Summer Institute for the Gifted and Talented
	Wilmington College
	Department of Education
	Pyle Center, Box 1293
	Wilmington, OH 45177
	(800) 341-9318 ext. 274

The Ohio Summer Institutes
for Gifted and Talented Students

Ohio provides its gifted and talented students with local opportunities for educational enrichment. Seven universities offer commuting students programs that challenge their imaginations and enhance their creativity. Students engage in an extensive study in a field of their choice. Each university provides its own assortment of courses. Some examples of these offerings include classes in law, health care, and the practice and ethics of medicine at the University of Cincinnati. Ohio State University offers an intensive arts program, a supercomputing course, and a course on the role of computers in engineering. Classes in theater, fiction writing, computer-aided product design, and art and computer graphics are available at the University of Toledo. Courses in architecture, creative writing, education, photography, and psychology are offered at Ohio University, and aviation, biomedical sciences, math, prelaw, and business are offered at Shawnee State. Youngstown State offers chemistry, journalism, physics, theater, and archaeology. Students can choose from offerings in musical theater, animation, visual arts, research and technology, and careers in cuisine at the University of Akron. Interested students should contact the program coordinator for current offerings. ***Application deadline: April 11.***

Host School:	Ohio colleges and universities
Type:	Selected Subjects
Location:	Held at selected sites around Ohio
Duration:	One to three weeks
Dates:	Assorted dates from late June through late July.
Qualifications:	Entering grades 10 and 11. Open to gifted and talented Ohio students who seek an educational enrichment experience during the summer.
Housing:	These are commuter programs. No housing is provided.
Costs:	No instructional costs. Students are responsible for transportation to and from the campus each day and lunch money.
Credits Given:	None
Contact:	John Herner
	The Ohio Summer Institutes for Gifted and Talented Students
	Department of Education, Division of Special Education
	933 High Street
	Worthington, OH 43085-4087
	(614) 466-2650

$\mathbb{P}$eaks & Potentials

Peaks & Potentials is designed to provide high-ability/high-potential students with the chance to explore topics in which they are interested. Two programs are offered, each directed to students in specific grade levels. Participants may choose from a list of topics that include television studio production, flight, using Hypercard, holography, acting, architecture, agriculture, and photography, as well as other subjects. All classes emphasize personal attention and small-group inter-action, as well as utilizing a hands-on approach to learning. Three workshops are offered daily. University students serve as counselors during the program. Evening activities include recreational sports such as archery, racquetball, tennis, and tae kwon do. *Rolling admissions; early registration is advised.*

Host School:	Montana State University
Type:	Comprehensive
Location:	Bozeman, MT
Duration:	One week.
Dates:	Peaks I is held in late June. Peaks II is held in mid-July.
Qualifications:	Entering grades 5 through 9. Peaks I is for students entering grades 5 through 7; Peaks II is for students entering grades 8 and 9.
Housing:	Optional housing is provided in double-occupancy dorm rooms. Residential students have their meals in the residence hall cafeteria. Commuter students are welcome.
Costs:	$165 for commuter students. Students who choose to reside on campus pay an additional room-and-board fee of $110.
Credits Given:	None
Contact:	Peaks & Potentials
	Montana State University
	Extended Studies
	204 Culbertson
	Bozeman, MT 59717
	(406) 994-4930

Principal's Scholars Summer Enrichment Program

The Principal's Scholars Summer Enrichment Program provides 100 students from participating schools around Illinois with the opportunity to get an early look at life as a college student while taking part in academic enrichment experiences. Mornings are devoted to classroom study in subjects that include English, mathematics, computer technology, science, and public speaking. Afternoons are spent in recreational activities including swimming, bowling, and roller skating. *Contact the program coordinator for application information and deadline.*

Host School:	University of Illinois, Urbana-Champaign
Type:	Comprehensive
Location:	Champaign, IL
Duration:	Four weeks
Dates:	Mid-July through early August
Qualifications:	Entering grade 11. Open to students from participating high schools throughout Illinois.
Housing:	Participants are housed in a dormitory and have meals in the dining hall.
Costs:	$50
Credits Given:	None
Contact:	Jacqueline Williams
	Principal's Scholars Summer Enrichment Program
	University of Illinois, Urbana-Champaign
	Office of Continuing Education and Public Service
	302 E. John Street, Suite 202
	Champaign, IL 61820
	(217) 333-0234

Service Civil International/International Voluntary Service (SCI/IVS) Workcamps

Today the Service Civil International (SCI), founded in 1920, has more than 5000 volunteers each year. Workcamps located in over 30 countries are designed to promote international understanding and peace through community service in the United States and abroad. Participants travel, learn about today's issues, and bring home with them memories of fun and hard work, and the satisfaction that comes from knowing that they have made a difference. Workcamps consist of 8 to 15 volunteers who come together to work on a meaningful project to solve problems, to learn from each other, and to share cooking and cleaning. Each workcamp has a local sponsor; these may be environmental groups, village councils, or a community of people with disabilities. Projects might include organizing children's activities, repairing fences at wildlife sanctuaries, renovating a shelter, educating people about pollution, or any of numerous other community service needs. Volunteers are placed on the workcamps of their choice on a first-registered, first-served basis after May 1. *Application deadline: rolling admissions.*

Host School:	SCI/IVS
Type:	Volunteer Service
Location:	Sites across the United States and abroad
Duration:	Two to three weeks
Dates:	Various dates, June through October
Qualifications:	Age 16 and older for United States camps; 18 and older for overseas camps.
Housing:	Housing and food for volunteers are provided at or near the workcamp site.
Costs:	$40 registration fee for U.S. camps; $80 registration fee for European camps. SCI provides room and board as well as supplemental health and accident insurance.
Credits Given:	None
Contact:	Service Civil International/International Voluntary Service (SCI/IVS) Workcamps
	SCI/IVS
	Route 2, Box 506
	Crozet, VA 22932
	(804) 823-1826

Student Conservation Association
High School Program

High School Work Group (HSP) participants spend four to five weeks completing outdoor work projects such as trail construction, wildlife habitat improvement, construction of shelters, and archaeological field survey work for government land management agencies, including the National Park Service, the United States Forest Service, Fish and Wildlife Service, the Bureau of Land Management, and others. Informal educational activities, including field identification and geology, discussions about environmental issues and ecological principles, and low-impact camping techniques, are part of the program. Recreational activities are available after work, and one week of each session is devoted to a recreational backpack or canoe trip. Participants have an opportunity to explore career options in the field of natural resources and are exposed to practical environmental education. *Application deadline: March 1.*

Host School:	Student Conservation Association, Inc. (SCA)
Type:	Volunteer Service
Location:	National sites
Duration:	Four to five weeks
Dates:	Varying dates, June through August
Qualifications:	The program is open to highschool students and graduating seniors who will be at least 16 years old by the end of the program. Positions are offered on a competitive basis.
Housing:	Participants are provided with camping accommodations. Meals are provided.
Costs:	No tuition costs. Food, lodging, and group equipment are provided. Participants are responsible for personal gear. Financial aid is available on an as-needed basis.
Credits Given:	None
Contact:	Student Conservation Association High School Program Student Conservation Association, Inc. (SCA) Box 550 Charleston, NH 03603 (603) 543-1700; FAX (603) 543-1828

Student Profile

Joshua Deutsch
Monsey, N.Y.
Student Conservation Association
High School Work Group
Josh participated in the High School Work Group project during the summer before his senior year.

I applied to the Student Conservation Association to gain a hold on a new experience, and by the end of the program the experience had a hold on me. I was assigned to be part of a six-person crew whose mission was to repair damaged land in Yosemite National Park, California. We were to take the first steps in restoring land that had been damaged by overuse and threatened by continued erosion.

My group was composed of three men, three women, and Nick, our group leader, guide, teacher, and friend. The members of my group came from all regions of the United States, representing five different religions and several ethnic backgrounds. We learned about each other through our daily labors and late-night conversations, and soon we found we were more alike than not.

Nick taught us methods of conservation, infusing in us the spirituality of our surroundings. He read to us each night and through his insight, wisdom, and example, taught us that individually we were an important part of nature, but as a whole, our group was a powerful force of change. Without each other we could not have survived. It became clear that others needed me as much as I needed them. It was this dependence that showed me I could be one of a whole and not lose myself.

We made our campsite in the backwoods of Tuolumne Meadows, a remote, isolated, northern region of the park. The eight hours of physical labor ahead of us did not seem to matter as we woke each morning to see a beauty that extended to the horizon, unmarred by buildings and freeways. The meadows rushed to meet mountains on every side, and on weekends, we would climb these peaks to be among the clouds. It was clear that I was a visitor to Tuolumne Meadows, the land belonging to those with fur and feathers rather than hiking boots and waterproof matches.

As I look back and reflect on the events of the summer program, I know it was unique. I was fortunate enough to find a program which promoted doing something good for ourselves in an awe-inspiring place. I remember the pool in Delaney Creek which served as our bathing hole, where I shed some of my reservedness. I remember the way the sun reflected off a high peak and into my eyes, filling me with wonderment. I remember the Giant's Table, a long rectangular slab of rock which looked like a sitting place for ancient kings. And I remember the hawk, which sat and watched our work each day to ensure we were doing it right.

I received a letter from Nick not too long ago after he visited our work site. He wrote, "I came to Delaney Creek. She was barely running. . . I walked past the Giant's Table and by the places where our tents and kitchen were set up. I walked by our work site. It looked so good. I remember rocks that we had placed, remembered trees we had planted. I walked from the west end of the trail to the dirt pits and continued on to look at next year's project and the year after that . . ." We had begun a long process that summer, a step on the road to healing and recovery for the land, and in the process, some of that revitalization found its way into me.

Summer Children's Programs

Louisiana State University in Shreveport offers an extensive array of summer programs for children of all ages. These programs meet during designated time periods on weekdays during the summer. The Summer Academy introduces students to the joy of learning; no tests or grades are given. Students may choose from a list of subjects including math, Italian, speed reading, writing, computers, criminology, and sign language. For creative problem solving and advanced learning, academically talented students might join the Summer Solstice program. The Youth Writing Project and the Youth Art Clinic provide experience to students seeking enrichment in writing and the arts. The Nature Day Camp offers science and craft activities, while the Children's Swim Program offers all levels of swimming instruction for students ages 2^1/2 to 18. Louisiana State even offers computer classes for kids and their parents, to help parents. ***Contact the Division of Continuing Education for more information.***

Host School:	Louisiana State University in Shreveport
Type:	Summer Enrichment Classes
Location:	Shreveport, LA
Duration:	One to three weeks
Dates:	Multiple sessions are offered beginning in early June and running through early August
Qualifications:	Students entering grades 3 through 12. Most of the programs are available on a first-come, first-served basis and are open to all interested students. The Summer Solstice program is limited to academically talented students with at least a B average.
Housing:	None. This is a commuter program for students residing in the Shreveport area.
Costs:	Classes range in price from about $50 to $195. The majority of offerings are less than $100. A limited number of partial scholarships are available on a need basis for several of the courses.
Credits Given:	None
Contact:	Summer Children's Programs
	Louisiana State University in Shreveport
	Conferences and Institutes
	Division of Continuing Education and Public Service
	One University Place
	Shreveport, LA 71115
	(318) 797-5262

Summer Scholars Program

Each summer, Saint Peter's College awards summer scholarships to seventy-five high school students. Participants experience life as a college student while participating in a challenging academic experience. Students may choose classes from the college course catalog, earning college credits for all work completed. Course selections include such subjects as principles of accounting, biology, biological ethics, chemistry, computers, micro- and macroeconomics, child psychology, education, literature, visual arts, music, photography, dance, Western civilization, mathematics, anthropology, foreign languages, philosophy, physics, psychology, sociology, religion, and political science. Entering 11th-grade students who successfully complete the program are invited back during the next summer. *Application deadline: March 2.*

Host School:	Saint Peter's College
Type:	Summer College Courses
Location:	Jersey City, NJ
Duration:	Five weeks
Dates:	Two sessions are offered: early June through early July and mid-July through mid-August.
Qualifications:	Entering grades 11 and 12. The program is open to motivated students who wish to challenge themselves with college-level summer courses.
Housing:	No housing is provided.
Costs:	No tuition fees are charged. Students may take one, two, or more courses during each of the two summer sessions.
Credits Given:	College credits are available upon successful completion of courses.
Contact:	Summer Scholars Program
	Saint Peter's College
	2641 Kennedy Boulevard
	Jersey City, NJ 07306
	(201) 915-9213

Telluride Association Summer Programs (TASP)

The Telluride Association Summer Programs (TASP) bring together a community of young people who share a passion for learning. In an extremely challenging, intellectually stimulating six weeks, students attend seminars, critically read and analyze texts, examine and discuss controversial ideas, and learn to express their ideas clearly, both orally and in writing. TASP participants attend small-group seminars three hours per day, focusing on chosen topics of exploration. One recent summer, students in the Cornell program studied "Poetry and the Body Politic," considering the power of art in our society, while those at St. John's College discussed the "Foundations of Modernity," studying the work of authors such as Machiavelli, Hobbes, Rousseau, Whitman, and Emily Dickinson. Intellectual pursuits also reach beyond the seminar rooms with students attending special guest lectures, presenting speeches on topics of interest, and joining in dinner-table and late-night discussions. Each TASP community meets as a group to plan activities and projects. Time is also set aside for informal activities, such as parties, movies, and participation in cultural and recreational events. Nomination letters must be received by December 21. **Application deadline: February 1.**

Host School:	Cornell University and St. Johns College
Type:	Comprehensive
Location:	Ithaca, NY, and Annapolis, MD
Duration:	Six weeks
Dates:	Late June through early August
Qualifications:	Entering grade 12. Students who have received PSAT scores within the top one percent may be considered for the program; other students may be nominated by a teacher or counselor who writes to the association.
Housing:	Participants are housed in dormitories at the host institution and have meals in the dining hall.
Costs:	None. Participants may request financial aid to cover reasonable travel costs.
Credits given:	None
Contact:	Telluride Association Summer Programs (TASP)
	Cornell University and St. John's College
	Telluride Association
	217 West Avenue
	Ithaca, NY 14850
	(607) 273-5011

Upward Bound Program: Iowa State

Upward Bound is a college preparatory program for low-income or first-generation college students. The program is designed to prepare participants for post-secondary education by providing academic, cultural, and social programs. The school year component consists of classes, tutoring, and workshops held on campus on Saturdays. Students are tutored in English, math, science, and social studies, and attend workshops that address a variety of topics including financial aid, college admissions testing preparation, college selection and admissions, and money management. During the summer sessions, students may choose to take part in a residential six-week Upward Bound program that includes classes in English, math, science, computer science, reading, and sessions on career and social awareness. Students may also take college classes during an eight-week summer session. The summer programs culminate with the students writing, producing, and directing a talent show. *Students are recruited from target-area middle schools in January and February and selected in May for a four-year commitment.*

Host School:	Iowa State University
Type:	Summer and Academic Year Enrichment Program
Location:	Ames, IA
Duration:	Six to eight weeks during the summer; on Saturdays during the school year.
Dates:	Summer (June through August) and academic year (September through May)
Qualifications:	Entering grades 9 through 12. Students must be from selected target school districts in Iowa. Eligible students come from low-income families or from families in which neither parent has a 4-year college degree. Students must also show potential and desire to attend and complete college.
Housing:	Participants are housed in dormitories and have meals in the dining halls.
Costs:	None. Participants are provided with a stipend of $15 per week during the summer session and with $10 per Saturday session during the school year when all requirements are met.
Credits Given:	None for Upward Bound classes; credits are given for regular college classes.
Contact:	Upward Bound Program: Iowa State
	Iowa State University
	Student Affairs Division
	N002 Lagomarcino Hall
	Ames, IA 50011-3187
	(515) 294-5471; FAX (515) 294-1219

Upward Bound: Michigan State

Upward Bound is a year-round program designed to motivate disadvantaged youth with academic potential. The program focuses on the development of the skills needed to succeed in postsecondary education. A six-week residential summer component provides personal and academic counseling. Students receive instruction in math, science, and computers, and they may take elective classes in drama, tennis, and communication skills. Career workshops present opportunities for future career exploration while additional tutoring increases mastery of basic skills. Field trips and numerous extracurricular activities complete the summer session. During the school year, students meet once a week for instruction and tutorial assistance by secondary school teachers, university faculty, and graduate and undergraduate college students. It is expected that Upward Bound participants will be more aware of college and career opportunities and eager to take advantage of options open to them. ***Contact program coordinator for application information.***

Host School:	Michigan State University
Type:	School Year and Summer Academic Enrichment Program
Location:	East Lansing, MI
Duration:	Once a week during the school year and a six-week residential summer program.
Dates:	Throughout the school year and mid-June to the end of July for the summer program.
Qualifications:	Students currently in grades 9 through 12. Open to low-income and potential first-generation college students from high schools in the greater Lansing area.
Housing:	Housing and meals are provided on campus during the summer residential portion of the program. The school year component is a commuter program.
Costs:	None. Students are provided with a stipend of $5 per week during the academic year and $10 per week during the summer.
Credits Given:	None
Contact:	Upward Bound: Michigan State
	Michigan State University
	276 Bessey Hall
	East Lansing, MI 48824
	(517) 353-6701

University of Wyoming Summer High School Institute

The University of Wyoming Summer High School Institute seeks to provide a well-balanced university experience for talented Wyoming students. The program is designed to challenge the students' imaginations to discover the excitement of learning. To stimulate creative thinking, students choose two interdisciplinary courses from a variety presented. Courses weave together such fields as English, economics, chemistry, sociology, philosophy, fine arts, psychology, nutrition, law, politics, and personal relationships. Course work includes class discussions, outside reading and research, and often the completion of a team project. Field trips and field research provide students with firsthand learning experiences. Recent course selections have included: "Immoral, but Not Illegal—or Is It?," a class which investigates hard choices through interesting and controversial topics; "Fission, Fusion, Psychosis: Our Entry into the Atomic Age," which explores the origin of the atomic age and the ethical questions that surround the subject; "Prometheus, Frankenstein, and *Star Trek:* The Problem of Modern Technology," which considers the ethical, political, personal, and philosophical issues raised by technology and technological change. In addition, all students also take the class "Living and Learning: Exploring Personal Relationships." An extensive program of cultural and social extracurricular activities are available to students. *Application deadline: March 1.*

Host School:	University of Wyoming
Type:	Comprehensive
Location:	Laramie, WY
Duration:	Three weeks
Dates:	Early through late June
Qualifications:	Entering grade 11. Open to talented Wyoming students committed to learning. Students are nominated by their schools.
Housing:	Participants are housed in a residence hall and have meals in the dining room.
Costs:	None
Credits Given:	None
Contact:	University of Wyoming Summer High School Institute
	University of Wyoming
	P.O. Box 4147
	218 Old Biochemistry Building
	Laramie, WY 82071
	(307) 766-3005

Vested Interest Program (VIP)

The Vested Interest Program (VIP) provides students with the opportunity to pursue further study in an area of special interest utilizing library research and report writing. All participants take the 3-credit course, Modes of Inquiry, which focuses on effective use of the university library and preparation of the research report. Students choose an additional college-level class from a selection that includes physiology, health science, computer programming, literature, and international perspectives. Foundations of Human Physiology surveys the organ systems of the human body and includes laboratory activities. Health Science introduces career options in medical laboratory science, occupational and physical therapy, and dietetics and nutrition. Computer Programming offers a hands-on study of computer application software such as word processing, spreadsheets, and database management. Approaches to Literature allows students to study significant authors and to explore the creative process. International Perspectives investigates topics that include population, nuclear weapons, human rights, and local politics. The forces at work in the international arena are studied, as well as their impact on the local area. Classes meet four mornings a week and are offered at both the north and south campuses. *Application deadline: May 16.*

Host School:	Florida International University
Type:	Selected Subjects
Location:	Miami, FL
Duration:	Six weeks
Dates:	End of June through mid-August
Qualifications:	Entering grade 12. The program is open to academically strong students interested in an early look at college life.
Housing:	Although this is primarily a commuter program, limited campus housing is available at student expense.
Costs:	None. Full tuition and a book stipend are awarded to each VIP student.
Credits Given:	6 to 7 college credits. Dual enrollment credits available to Dade County students.
Contact:	Ms. Caryl Grof
	Vested Interest Program (VIP)
	Florida International University
	University Park, DM 368
	Miami, FL 33199
	(305) 348-4100

Student Profile

Joy Basewiez
Miami, Fla.
Vested Interest Program
Joy, 17, was a VIP participant during the summer before her senior year.

This past summer I participated in the Vested Interest Program (VIP) at Florida International University. It was definitely a worthwhile way to spend my summer. This intensive six-week program gave me the opportunity to experience a college atmosphere while taking two college-level courses.

The first course I took was Modes of Inquiry, a fast-paced English class. The teacher encouraged us to ask questions and have discussions. The friendly, receptive environment which characterized this class gave me the confidence to probe my personal understanding of different issues that are important today. At the same time it gave me the unique opportunity to develop my opinions and share them with others. By the end of this course I noticed that I was a lot more confident when it came to writing and research.

For the second course, a student is able to choose from a wide variety of topics. Every student will be able to find a course which suits their specific interests. I took a computer course in which I was introduced to the basics of computer software and programs. We each had access to individual computers, as well as to the computer labs. I was able to practice and to do my work on any one of the many state-of-the-art computers available. If I ever had any problems I was able to ask any of the supervisors in the lab for assistance.

In addition, one of the best features of this program was the people. Since we commuted from home every day, most of the students in the VIP lived in the area and we got the chance to get together outside of classes. We even kept in touch after the classes were over.

The VIP program was great. I recommend it to any rising high school senior or college freshman interested in a summer of learning and meeting a variety of people.

Virginia Governor's Schools Summer Regional Schools

The state of Virginia sponsors regional Governor's Schools in more than 20 areas of the state each summer. These programs are designed to meet the needs of the regions' gifted elementary, middle school, or high school students. They provide exciting opportunities in the arts, sciences, and humanities. The programs are generally located at a public school or on a college or university campus. Program topics vary from year to year, but a recent summer's programs included such offerings as art and ideas, environmental studies, ecology, technology, vocational studies, humanities/arts and science, science/math/writing, science, and math/science/drama. ***Contact program director or local school gifted coordinator for upcoming summer offerings and application information.***

Host School:	Department of Education and participating public school divisions
Type:	Selected Subjects
Location:	Various sites across Virginia
Duration:	Two to four weeks
Dates:	June and July
Qualifications:	Entering grades 3 through 12. Open to gifted and talented Virginia residents.
Housing:	These are nonresidential programs, held in locations near the participants' homes.
Costs:	No program costs. Students are responsible for their own lunches.
Credits Given:	None
Contact:	Dr. Janie Craig
	Virginia Governor's Schools Summer Regional Schools
	Department of Education
	101 N. 14th Street
	Richmond, VA 23219
	(804) 225-2884; FAX (804) 786-5466

Volunteer Trail Crews

Each summer, volunteer crews head into the woods or to the top of America's oldest mountain range to construct, rebuild, or repair parts of the legendary Appalachian Trail. Participants have a chance to work outdoors, honing outdoor skills, and enjoy the camaraderie of volunteers of all ages and from all walks of life. All trail crews concentrate on trail construction and resource-management projects to assist and support local clubs and public agencies. Sites include national and state forests and parks. The work is physically challenging and includes trail design and construction, shelter and bridge construction, rough carpentry, clearing, and open-areas management. The lifestyle is rustic. Trail crews of six to eight volunteers are guided by a skilled leader on projects, returning to the base camp for two-day breaks each week. Base camp facilities are designed for a comfortable time off. This is a challenging program for those who love the outdoors and who wish to give something back to an area they have enjoyed. **Contact the ATC office for more information about current work projects.**

Host School:	The Appalachian Trail Conference (ATC)
Type:	Volunteer Service
Location:	Selected sites along the Appalachian Trail from Maine to Georgia
Duration:	One week to a full season
Dates:	Summer
Qualifications:	Open mainly to volunteers 18 and older, but 16- and 17-year-old students with good references and lots of outdoor experience are also welcome. Volunteers should be enthusiastic, adaptable, and in good physical condition.
Housing:	Volunteers live in rustic conditions at the worksite, often at developed or primitive tent camp sites. Some crews are housed in cabins. Meals are provided. Volunteers need to supply their own basic camping gear.
Costs:	No cost while on the program.
Credits Given:	None
Contact:	Volunteer Trail Crews
	The Appalachian Trail Conference (ATC)
	ATC Regional Office
	P.O. Box 10
	Newport, VA 24128
	(703) 544-7388; (304) 535-6331

Volunteer Trails Program

The Appalachian Mountain Club (AMC) offers volunteers from ages 12 to over 65 an opportunity to engage in hard work amid spectacular scenery and to make a lasting personal contribution toward the protection and management of our natural resources. The AMC Trails program is committed to the maintenance of the Appalachian Trail, teaching volunteers how to design, build, and maintain a trail. Trails skills seminars include instruction on chain-saw use. Volunteer crews spend their time working in national forests, parks, and wilderness areas in Alaska, Montana, Wyoming, Maine, and Idaho. Other weeklong programs take volunteers to the Catskill Preserve in New York State, to AMC's Bascom Lodge atop Mt. Greylock in the Berkshire Mountains of Massachusetts, and to the White Mountains in New Hampshire. AMC also offers volunteers of all ages opportunities for weekend participation programs, as well as trails skills development courses. ***Contact the program for program opportunities and dates.***

Host School:	Appalachian Mountain Club
Type:	Volunteer Service
Location:	National and state parks and forests across the United States
Duration:	One week to ten days
Dates:	Throughout the summer
Qualifications:	Age 16 for service trips and volunteer crews. Younger volunteers may be accepted if accompanied by an adult.
Housing:	Lodging and meals are provided. Participants camp out during the backcountry portions of the workcamp.
Costs:	Costs range from $30 to $195 depending upon the program selected. Fees include tools, training, lodging, and meals.
Credits Given:	None
Contact:	Volunteer Trails Program
	Appalachian Mountain Club
	P.O. Box 298
	Gorham, NH 03581
	(413) 443-0011

The West Virginia Governor's Honors Academy

Classes at the Governor's Honors Academy are offered in a variety of areas, including the arts, humanities, and math and science. Students take an intensive morning class in their field of interest. Because the Governor's Honors Academy favors a holistic view of education, participants also take a broad-based afternoon class that must be chosen from outside the student's own field. Thus, a science student might spend his afternoon in a pottery class. A unique feature of the West Virginia program is the "group." The group meets three days a week, with students discussing topics of their choice in a safe, caring environment. College preparatory sessions three times per week provide information about the college admissions test preparation, college selection, application, and financial aid process. Teachers often offer special short enrichment courses in their subject areas for students who were unable to take their class during one of the intensive periods. This gives participants a chance to explore still other areas of learning. Recreational activities, or "forced fun," take place before dinner each evening. Special events are planned for each night of the program and include such activities as poetry readings, guest speakers, orchestral performances, and dances. A two-day, small-group field trip to Washington, D.C., finds students spending significant time in places of their own choosing. *Application deadline: February 15.*

Host School:	West Virginia State College
Type:	Comprehensive
Location:	Institute, WV
Duration:	Four weeks
Dates:	July
Qualifications:	Entering grade 12. Excellent students (as measured by both standardized test scores and grades) from every county in West Virginia are eligible for the program.
Housing:	Participants are housed in dormitories and have meals in the dining hall.
Costs:	None
Credits Given:	None
Contact:	Dr. Virginia Simmons
	The West Virginia Governor's Honors Academy
	West Virginia Department of Education
	Building 6, Room 362, Capitol Complex
	Charleston, WV 25305-0330
	(304) 558-0160; FAX (304) 558-0048

Part Two: School Year Adventures

A wide variety of enrichment programs are available to students to enhance school year experiences. Participating in these opportunities can help you to understand the real-world applications of concepts studied in school. Academic year enrichment programs are especially important for those students whose home schools provide limited exposure to hands-on education. Unless your school offers unlimited access to science laboratories, writing centers, and computing and technology equipment, or provides numerous opportunities for immersion in the visual and performing arts, you'll find that supplementing your school's program with academic year enrichment will add greatly to your education.

Academic year adventures come in various forms. Each type of program presents opportunities to expand your knowledge and to gain practical experience. Enrichment experiences include:

Internships and apprenticeships

Enrichment classes and workshops

Distance-learning opportunities

School-break programs

Volunteer involvement

Accelerated programs

A word of caution first: Students contemplating involvement with a school year enrichment program should be aware that the time to participate in these programs must be carved out of an already busy week. Good time-management skills are needed to juggle school work with extracurricular, social, family, and recreational obligations, as well as to find time to take part in these enrichment programs. Is it worth it? For those of you who always want to learn a little more, for those who want to get the most out high school, and for those who seek more contact with a field they feel passionate about, academic year enrichment programs pay off handsomely in terms of both experience and knowledge gained.

Internships and Apprenticeships

Internships and apprenticeships provide the most intensive of all hands-on experiences. Participating in an internship program is perhaps the best way of determining if a particular career is right for you. During an internship, the student is paired with a mentor, generally a practicing professional in a field of the student's interest. The mentor provides guidance, advice, and support. The mentor also directs the student's learning through involvement in a project or research activity. Students taking part in science internships might join an established research team and participate in one aspect of an ongoing project, or they might initiate their own independent study, relying on their mentors for guidance as needed. Art apprentices assist their mentor in the studio, learning new techniques and expanding their skills as they work. In all cases, students who take part in an internship or apprenticeship develop a true understanding of the real-world applications of their studies.

How can a student get involved in an internship or apprenticeship? Your home school may have an established internship program. Consult your guidance counselor or the appropriate subject area teacher to find out if you can become involved in an ongoing internship program through your home school or school district.

Mentors for school-based programs are usually found through college and university contacts and by association with local industries and community organizations. Regional hospitals, local theaters, television stations, newspapers, art museums, professional offices and career organizations, and area businesses all serve as sources of mentors. If your school does not offer an internship program, contact your State Department of Education or the subject coordinator at your local school district office for help in locating a local mentor.

Young women or members of minority groups can check with appropriate community organizations to see if they sponsor internships for members. Many organizations, such as the Mid-America Consortium for Engineering and Science Achievement (MACESA) and groups associated with the National Association of Precollege Directors (NAPD) provide student internship opportunities. Local chapters of professional organizations such as medical and dental societies, the American Chemical Society, the National Society of Public Accountants, the American Bar Association, and the National Association of Broadcasters may also support student internship programs.

Private industries and local businesses are also good sources of internship opportunities; IBM, through its "Problem-solving Project Mentor's Program," provides mentors, laboratory facilities, and materials for student research. The Minnesota Artist Mentor Program, described later in this chapter, is a good example of how a state can provide apprenticeship opportunities for talented students.

Students can also initiate their own internship or apprenticeship. They may contact the author of an article or book that addresses their subject of interest, and begin ongoing communication with that individual. Keep in mind that by utilizing varied forms of communication, from "snail mail" to e-mail, the telephone to the Internet, mentors can be drawn from individuals around the world. Often, people who feel strongly about their field of work are happy to share their ideas and advice with young people who share their interest.

When taking part in an internship or apprenticeship, it is important that both the student and mentor be realistic in their expectations about the relationship. Students should expect to be on-site at the agreed-upon times, and to conduct themselves in a businesslike manner. Students can be expected to contribute to ongoing work at the mentor's workplace, be it a studio, laboratory, or office. Internships and apprenticeships provide a firsthand look at the life of a practicing professional and can be a very rewarding experience for both the student and mentor.

Enrichment Classes and Workshops

Although some larger high schools can offer an array of elective classes, many schools are unable to provide more than basic courses and a few popular elective choices. To supplement the courses available at their home schools, students might consider taking part in alternative educational opportunities.

Local colleges and universities often allow qualified students to take college-level courses though dual high school/college enrollment. For example, students in Dade County, Florida, may utilize the dual enrollment program to complete a year or more of college classes while still in high school. Students might also avail themselves of opportunities presented through continuing education offerings at these institutions and expand their minds through courses taken just for fun. You might choose a class in "Accessing the Information Superhighway" or one in "Starting Your Own Small Business."

Your area college or university might also offer special workshops and presentations. For example, Gustavus Adolphus College invites 11th- and 12th-grade students to campus each year for their Nobel Conference. These precollege students have an opportunity to listen to and interact with noted experts and Nobel laureates. Iowa's ACES (Academically Challenging Experiences on Saturdays) program offers enrichment opportunities for both local students on campus and to out-of-state students through a correspondence course. Many other programs are described in this chapter.

Distance-Learning Opportunities

Distance learning provides still additional options for free or low-cost educational enrichment. The Boston Museum of Science offers "Science-by-Mail," linking student teams with volunteer scientist pen pals. The scientists provide encouragement and advice to small groups of students attempting to find solutions to a scientific challenge.

More traditional distance-learning courses may be arranged through correspondence school. This offers students a chance to supplement their own school's curriculum through independent study. In this way, students can study subjects their school is unable to provide, and may earn high school or college credit for their work. Through correspondence courses offered by the American School, the University of Tennessee, the University of Florida, and other institutions, students work at their own pace, following a curriculum that includes readings, assignments, and exams.

"High-tech" programs take advantage of the "information superhighway," linking students and instructors through the use of computers, modems, and interactive television. Small groups of students from schools across the state or across the country can take part in specialized offerings, or be taught by professionals renowned in their fields. Individual students may enhance their writing skills through programs that utilize the Internet. Access to a satellite dish at either school or home provides still more options for distance learning. Young people with only access to regular television may still enhance their education through network television and PBS offerings. In recent seasons, ongoing PBS programs have included "Scientific American's Frontiers," "The New Explorers", and "Newton's Apple."

School-Break Adventures

Vacation periods and long weekends during the school year provide time for more intensive learning experiences. A number of universities and science institutes and art centers offer short courses and workshops during the winter or spring break. The White Mountain Archaeological Center provides hands-on archaeological experiences allowing young people to get a firsthand look at archaeological careers while learning about prehistoric people. The Pocono Environmental Center offers art and environmental science workshops, many open to both students and their families. Young artists might wish to participate in the Art Weekend Workshops at Savannah College of Art and Design, while budding writers can hone their literary skills at Michigan State's Young Writers' Workshop. Check with institutions in your region for similar programs.

Volunteer Involvement

Students can also enrich their academic year study through volunteer involvement with community-based, state, or national organizations. Environmental groups such as Earthwatch and Greenpeace welcome student volunteers, as do political parties, museums, and cultural organizations. Besides providing these groups with much-needed help, students meet other members who share similar interests and have an opportunity to develop a network of professional contacts.

Volunteering permits students to get a close look at career opportunities. Young people interested in the health sciences might volunteer their time at area hospitals or community health centers. Aspiring veterinarians can offer their services at the ASPCA, or other animal protection agency, or provide help at a local animal hospital or shelter. If you're interested in a career in journalism or broadcast media, you might submit an article to a community newspaper, or offer your help to a public access radio or TV station. Working with a literacy program will help students planning a career in education discover if this is the field for them. In addition to the knowledge you'll gain about careers, volunteering can bolster your resume, provide letters of recommendation from individuals very familiar with your work, and may enhance your chance for admission to a selective college or university.

Accelerated Programs

Accelerated programs allow students to delve more deeply into a subject at a pace faster than that of traditional courses of study. Students in accelerated programs also have the advantage of being with highly motivated peers. Accelerated enrichment programs may be offered during the school year as a supplement to the standard curriculum. Michigan State University's CHAMP program provides mathematically gifted students with the opportunity to complete the traditional four years of high school math in two years. The Fernbank Science Center offers accelerated science programs that permit students to engage in intensive science studies in physics, biology, aerospace, or environmental science for interested Georgia students.

High school sophomores and juniors seeking academic challenges that their home schools are unable to provide may choose to enter college through an early admission program. Many colleges and universities offer admission to mature, motivated students who have not completed the traditional four years of high school. These openings are generally reserved for students who have exhausted the educational offerings of their local school.

The Acceleration to Excellence Program of Simon's Rock College of Bard is unique in that all of the college's students enter after their sophomore or junior year in high school. Unlike other early admission programs, students at Simon's Rock are surrounded by highly motivated peers of the same age and stage of development. Students in this program take an interdisciplinary course of studies and may complete their college education at Bard or transfer to another institution at the end of their first two years of study.

The listings that follow are representative of enrichment programs that operate during the academic year. Although these are often designed for local students, similar programs are likely to be found in many communities across the country. If you cannot find programs of interest in your community, you might wish to establish new ones based on those you read about here. Contact the program directors for more information. Seek out these free and low-cost opportunities; they will enrich your life!

School Year Programs

Academically Challenging Experiences on Saturdays (ACES)

Gifted students taking part in the Academically Challenging Experiences on Saturdays (ACES) program may choose from a selection of intellectually challenging courses. Literature and Composition is a correspondence course designed to give participants more practice with reading and writing than they may be getting in their home school. Every two weeks, students receive a packet of readings including stories, poems, and essays. A journal entry is made for each reading, and then a more polished writing assignment is submitted. Students get their assignments returned with comments and suggestions for revision and new packets to continue with their educational growth. A math course component diagnoses a student's understanding of mathematical concepts and individualizes course work to student needs. The instruction focuses on mastery of fundamental concepts, problem-solving skills, and independent learning. A third course offering in computer science also diagnostically tests the individual needs and abilities of participants and concentrates on necessary skills. Students can experience a wide variety of computer applications, including word processing, database management, spreadsheets, C-language programming, and mainframe computer interfacing. ***Contact program coordinator for application deadline.***

Host School:	Iowa State University
Type:	Academic Enrichment Classes
Location:	Various university sites in Iowa. Literature and Composition is a correspondence course.
Duration:	One semester
Dates:	Fall or spring semesters
Qualifications:	Students in grades 7 through 12. The program is open to academically gifted students who wish to develop their abilities in challenging academic areas. The Literature and Composition course is open to out-of-state students.
Housing:	None.
Costs:	$100 per semester for Literature and Composition. $200 per semester for math and computer science.
Credits Given:	High school credit may be available.
Contact:	Academically Challenging Experiences on Saturdays (ACES) Iowa State University W172 Lagomarcino Hall Ames, IA 50011-3180 (515) 294-1772 or (800) 262-3810 (ext. 1772)

Academy of American Poets
High School Writers Program

Columbia University writing students serve as instructors and role models for high school poets who wish to strengthen their writing skills. Students from schools across New York City come together on Saturday afternoons for this intensive poetry writing workshop. Students are given poems to read and consider, discussing the poetry as well as the technical issues during the workshops. Students also work on writing assignments each week, then read and discuss their own and other students' work. These small-group workshops provide a great deal of interaction between young poets and allow for individual attention. Informal discussions focus on technical writing skills as well as opportunities for publication. Instructors and participants share their experiences with each other; opportunities for further involvement in the literary world are also discussed. *Contact the program coordinator for dates of next workshop.*

Host School:	Academy of American Poets
Type:	Poetry Writing Workshops
Location:	New York, NY
Duration:	Six weeks, one Saturday afternoon per week
Dates:	Two sessions are offered in the spring.
Qualifications:	Grades 9 through 12. The program is open to any high school student interested in poetry writing.
Housing:	None. This is a commuter workshop.
Costs:	$60 for the six week program. Need-based scholarships are available.
Credits Given:	None
Contact:	Academy of American Poets High School Writers Program
	Academy of American Poets
	584 Broadway, Suite 1208
	New York, NY 10012-3250
	(212) 274-0343

The Acceleration to Excellence Scholarship Program

Simon's Rock College of Bard is the nation's only liberal arts college specifically designed for students of high school age. All students enter after their sophomore or junior year in high school; classes are filled with bright, talented students seeking academic challenges their high schools are unable to provide. The Acceleration to Excellence Scholarship Program offers full two-year college scholarships (valued at over $50,000) to a select group of these young people. Unlike other early admission programs, all students at Simon's Rock are "younger scholars" and thus surrounded by a peer group of intellectually oriented students at a similar stage of development. All entering students attend an intensive, weeklong workshop in writing and critical thinking before the first semester begins. A low student-faculty ratio, weekly adviser-advisee meetings, and a large adult presence in the dormitories ensure the personal contact and support needed by younger students. Students choose courses from a required core curriculum in addition to numerous elective offerings. Upon completing the two-year AA (Associate of Arts) degree, students may continue at Simon's Rock or at Bard College, at the same tuition as that charged by the state university system in their home state, or may transfer to another institution to complete their degree. *Application deadline: February 5.*

Host School:	Simon's Rock College of Bard
Type:	Academic Year Acceleration to College Program
Location:	Great Barrington, MA
Duration:	Two years
Dates:	Fall and spring semesters
Qualifications:	Students presently in grade 10. Applicants must have a grade point average of at least 3.3 (out of 4.0) and have shown "sustained effort and achievement" in at least one extracurricular activity.
Housing:	Participants are housed in dormitories and have meals in the dining hall.
Costs:	None. Scholarships cover the full cost of tuition, room, and board for two years of attendance at Simon's Rock.
Credits Given:	Two full years of college credits.
Contact:	The Acceleration to Excellence Scholarship Program
	Simon's Rock College of Bard
	Office of Academic Affairs
	84 Alford Road
	Great Barrington, MA 01230-9702
	(413) 528-7229; FAX (413) 528-7365

Art Weekend Workshops

The Savannah College of Art and Design offers a variety of weekend workshops to students interested in the visual arts. Fall Workshop Weekend, held each year in late October, offers students two art workshops chosen from the following departments: building arts, painting, illustration, computer art, graphic design, fashion, fibers, metals and jewelry, sequential art, and video. Campus tours, portfolio reviews, admissions counseling, and a Costume Ball complete this busy day that runs from 8 A.M. until midnight. The Comic Arts Forum in May presents interested high school students with the opportunity to expand their knowledge and understanding of sequential art. Professional comic artists conduct workshops, demonstrations, portfolio reviews, panel discussions, and slide shows. Workshop sessions are offered in pencils, inks, painting, coloring/computer, writing/storytelling, and life drawing for comics. *Contact the college for registration information for these and other special events.*

Host School:	Savannah College of Art and Design
Type:	Visual Arts Workshops
Location:	Savannah, GA
Duration:	One day
Dates:	Saturdays in October and May
Qualifications:	The program is open to high school juniors and seniors interested in the visual arts.
Housing:	Housing is available at special rates at selected area hotels. Some meals are provided on campus.
Costs:	Registration is $25 for the Fall Workshop Weekend program and includes two meals, two workshops, and admission to the Costume Ball. The Comic Arts Forum has a registration fee of $35, which includes two lunches and all forum activities and events.
Credits Given:	None
Contact:	Director of Special Events
	Art Weekend Workshops
	Savannah College of Art and Design
	342 Bull Street
	P.O. Box 3146
	Savannah, GA 31402-3146
	(800) 869-7223 or (912) 238-2483; FAX (912) 238-2456

Arts and Environmental Education Workshops

The Pocono Environmental Education Center (PEEC), in cooperation with the National Park Service, is the largest residential center in the Western Hemisphere for environmental education. Situated in the Delaware Water Gap recreation area, the Center is easily accessible from New Jersey and the greater New York and Philadelphia metropolitan areas. PEEC offers a variety of weekend programs throughout the year. Although the focus of the workshops may differ, all leave the participants with a greater understanding of, and appreciation for, our natural environment. Several of the weekends feature outdoor activities; a Backpacking Weekend and a Pocono Paddling Weekend introduce beginners to these skill areas. Walkers Weekends feature an appreciation of spring wildflowers or fall foliage, while the Storytelling Workshop focuses on this age-old art and imparts storytelling techniques. There is even a Bats in Your Belfry workshop, providing participants with a rare opportunity to learn about these essential animals. ***Contact PEEC for more information about all of their educational offerings.***

Host School:	Pocono Environmental Education Center
Type:	Environmental Education Workshops
Location:	Dingmans Ferry, PA
Duration:	Three days
Dates:	Weekend programs are offered throughout the year.
Qualifications:	Most programs are open to participants of all ages; families are encouraged to attend together. Some of the programs are designed for specific populations, such as teens or educators.
Housing:	Participants are housed in rustic single-room cabins which sleep from 2 to 6 people and include a full bathroom. Meals are served buffet style in the dining hall.
Costs:	$84 to $114 depending upon program selected.
Credits Given:	None
Contact:	Arts and Environmental Education Workshops
	Pocono Environmental Education Center
	RR 2, Box 1010
	Dingmans Ferry, PA 18328
	(717) 828-2319

CHAMP: Cooperative Highly Accelerated Mathematics Program

CHAMP provides mathematically gifted students with the opportunity to complete the traditional four years of high school math in two years. Students selected for the program meet one afternoon a week for two and one-half hours on the Michigan State campus. The curriculum and pacing of the course provide suitable challenge. Students also have the opportunity to interact with other highly gifted young people. During the first year of CHAMP, students study the equivalent of Algebra I and II. These courses emphasize basic algebraic skills and concepts, and higher-level problem solving and proof. The second year of CHAMP finds students studying geometry for one semester, followed by a precalculus course. The geometry course also emphasizes problem solving and proof, while the precalculus class includes college algebra and trigonometry. Students who complete the program are well prepared for a university-level calculus course. *Contact program coordinator for application information.*

Host School:	Michigan State University
Type:	Accelerated Mathematics Program
Location:	East Lansing, MI
Duration:	Two years, meeting one afternoon per week
Dates:	School year
Qualifications:	The program is open to middle and high school students, highly gifted in mathematics, who live in Clinton County, Eaton, and Ingham Intermediate School Districts in Michigan.
Housing:	None. Students commute to the campus for classes.
Costs:	$125 payable by the school districts, and/or parents.
Credits Given:	Four high school credits
Contact:	CHAMP: Cooperative Highly Accelerated Mathematics Program
	Michigan State University
	Office of Gifted and Talented Programs
	The Honors College
	East Lansing, MI 48824
	(517) 336-2129

CmPS: Community Problem Solving

Students who take part in Community Problem Solving have an opportunity to use problem-solving skills to tackle existing real-world problems. Student teams identify a problem that exists within the school, local, state, national, or world community, utilizing the Future Problem Solving process to reach a solution. They then develop and implement a plan of action. Through this program, students develop teamwork skills, learn and use problem-solving strategies, discover the relationship between goal setting and goal fulfillment, and become familiar with local, state, and federal agencies as information sources. Students discover the impact their efforts can have on the world around them as they bridge the gap between school and active community involvement. Completed project reports are sent to the International Office in the spring for judging. The top projects in each division are awarded $500 grants to offset the cost of travel to the International FPSP Conference in June. Past winners have promoted community recycling programs, led a restoration project for the battleship *Texas*, and adopted a local nursing/retirement home. Both the students involved and the community benefit from this enrichment activity.

Host School: University of Michigan

Type: Team Problem-Solving Program

Location: Program takes place at the student's home school.

Duration: School year

Dates: Teams work throughout school year and submit results in the spring.

Qualifications: Students may participate in one of three divisions. Junior division students are from grades 4 through 6; intermediate division includes grades 7 through 9; senior division is for grades 10 through 12. Teams may consist of any number of students working with a coach.

Housing: None. Program is conducted in the student's community.

Costs: $55 team registration. Fee includes all materials needed for participation, a subscription to the Future Problem-Solving Program (FPSP) Newsletter, staff assistance, access to informational and training workshops, and a written evaluation of completed project.

Credits Given: None

Contact: CmPS: Community Problem Solving
University of Michigan
Future Problem-Solving Program
318 West Ann Street
Ann Arbor, MI 48104-1337
(313) 998-7377

Educard

Educard is a special community program that gives any student interested in learning the chance to attend selected classes at Southern Illinois University at Edwardsville. Students can sample freely any of the subjects that interest them, from accounting to zoology. It is designed to provide an economical and flexible opportunity for individuals to experience professional growth and personal enrichment. No grades are given for Educard classes, nor are records of classwork or attendance kept; no transcript of these classes can be issued. However, Educard provides community members with a chance to explore any subject that is of interest. It is an opportunity to discover a new love for learning and, for students, the chance of finding a lifelong interest or possible career. *Contact the program office for registration information.*

Host School: Southern Illinois University at Edwardsville
Type: College Level Enrichment Courses
Location: Edwardsville, IL
Duration: One or more semesters
Dates: Fall, spring, or summer semesters
Qualifications: Educard is open to high school students at least 16 years of age, as well as anyone else interested in learning, who is not currently enrolled for credit in the university. Students may take up to three courses through Educard.
Housing: None. This is a commuter program.
Costs: $35 per course. Textbooks may be borrowed free of charge from the Textbook Service.
Credits Given: None
Contact: Educard
                      Southern Illinois University at Edwardsville
                      Office of Continuing Education
                      Rendleman 1330
                      Edwardsville, IL 62026
                      (618) 692-3210

Hands-On Archaeological Experience

White Mountain is operated as an archaeological field school and is dedicated to the research, preservation, and protection of prehistoric Southwest Indian sites. Current excavation takes place at the Raven Site Ruin, a five-acre site overlooking the Little Colorado River. Artifacts at this site are from the Mogollon and Anasazi Indian cultures and date back over 800 years. Participants help in excavation, working alongside professional archaeologists as they analyze, document, and restore the sites. Visitors hike or ride horseback into the canyons to survey and explore the surrounding area to better understand how the total environment was used by the prehistoric cultures. Some participants might choose to restore prehistoric ceramics, while others are adept at finding new petroglyph areas. Those visitors who stay for a week or more assume intensive archaeological field responsibilities and may choose to participate in more laboratory restorations. Staff archaeologists present evening lectures describing current and previous work or explain archaeological techniques. This is a good experience for students considering future careers in archaeology. ***Contact program for available dates.***

Host School:	White Mountain Archaeological Center
Type:	School Break Field Experience
Location:	St. Johns, AZ
Duration:	Programs range from day trips to overnight experiences to weeklong field programs.
Dates:	Mid-April through mid-October
Qualifications:	Open to people of all ages interested in archaeology. Participants may attend as individuals or as part of family or school groups, or special-interest clubs.
Housing:	Bunkhouse lodging and meals are provided on site for multiday programs. RV and tent camping as well as motel accommodations are also available nearby.
Costs:	Day rates: students (to age 17), $24; adults, $42. Fee includes program and lunch. Overnight rates: students, $44; adults, $66. Includes lodging, meals, and program.
Credits Given:	None
Contact:	A Hands-On Archaeological Experience
	White Mountain Archaeological Center
	HC 30
	St. Johns, AZ 85936
	(602) 333-5857

High School Credits by Independent Study

The American School offers challenging courses, summer school opportunities, and make-up credits by correspondence to high school students throughout the United States. The program provides instructional service (including unlimited consultations and personalized grading by qualified teachers), standard textbooks, study guides, and all educational materials needed to complete a particular course of study. Students may enroll in courses required for high school graduation, such as English, French, Spanish, mathematics, science, and social studies, or may choose elective and enrichment offerings. Classes are available in a variety of subjects that include computer awareness, automotive repair, carpentry, building trades, business, drafting, electricity, art, photography, and home living courses (child care, consumer economics, food study, home repairs). Upon completion of the course, students take a final exam proctored by an individual at the student's home school.

Host School: American School

Type: School Year Enrichment and Required High School Classes

Location: Student's home

Duration: Five weeks to one year

Dates: Students may begin at any time during the year.

Qualifications: The program is available to all interested students. Prior approval of the student's principal or guidance counselor is needed if high school credits are desired.

Housing: Student's home

Costs: From $52 for a $\frac{1}{2}$-credit course to a maximum of $154 for a 1-credit class. Fees include all needed textbooks and materials.

Credits Given: 1 or $\frac{1}{2}$ high school credit for successfully completed classes

Contact: Tom Kennelly
High School Credits by Independent Study
American School
850 East 58th Street
Chicago, IL 60637
(312) 947-3300

Independent Study by Correspondence

The University of Tennessee is representative of the many universities that offer a wide variety of enrichment as well as basic high school and college required classes to students across the country through correspondence study. Students may begin a class at any time, studying at a pace that meets their needs and lifestyle. Course work includes a series of reading and writing assignments that students complete, mail to the university for grading and comments, and have returned to them for review. At the end of the course, students take a final exam at a testing center in their area. High school credit classes available include required classes such as English, mathematics (arithmetic, algebra I and II, geometry, trigonometry), science (biology and physical science), social studies (civics, economics, government, U. S. history, world geography, world history), and foreign languages (French, Latin, Spanish). Elective enrichment offerings include cartooning, business education (accounting, business law, business math, office procedures), health, home economics, journalism, psychology, and sociology. Noncredit offerings in subjects that include computers, cartooning, nursing, and personal development as well as a full range of college credit courses are also available by correspondence.

Host School:	University of Tennessee
Type:	School Year Enrichment Courses and High School and College Credit Classes
Location:	Student's home
Duration:	Eight weeks to nine months
Dates:	School year
Qualifications:	The program is open to all interested students. Students interested in obtaining high school credit for independent study must secure the approval of their school administrators.
Housing:	These are correspondence courses mailed to the student's home.
Costs:	$57 for a one-semester high school course. College credit courses cost $73 per semester hour. Noncredit courses begin at $75 a course. Textbooks are additional.
Credits Given:	High school and college credits are available.
Contact:	Division of Continuing Education
	Independent Study by Correspondence
	University of Tennessee
	Department of Independent Study
	420 Communications Building
	Knoxville, TN 37996
	(615) 974-5134

Independent Study by Correspondence and Distance Education

The University of Florida in cooperation with the P. K. Yonge Laboratory School offers high school students the opportunity to take high school and college credit courses by correspondence. Students work at their own pace completing assigned readings and written assignments and mailing them to an instructor at the university. Assignments are graded and returned along with the instructor's comments. Midterm and final exams are proctored by the student's principal or guidance counselor at the student's school. A number of the courses offered have been awarded a distinguished or meritorius course award by the National University Continuing Education Association (NUCEA). Examples of course offerings include art, health management, humanities, English, Spanish, mathematics (from pre-algebra through algebra II, plus courses in informal geometry and business math), peer counseling, physical science, environmental science, social studies, and accounting. Students may also elect to take college credit courses chosen from a selection of lower-division university courses.

Host School:	University of Florida
Type:	School Year Enrichment Courses and Required High School and College Credit Courses
Location:	Student's home
Duration:	One month to one year
Dates:	Students may begin study at any time.
Qualifications:	The program is open to interested high school students. Students who wish to receive high school credit for their work must first obtain the approval of their principal or counselor.
Housing:	Student's home
Costs:	$110 per semester credit for high school credit classes. The cost of textbooks is additional.
Credits Given:	High school and college credits are available
Contact:	Independent Study by Correspondence and Distance Education University of Florida Division of Continuing Education, Suite D 2209 NW 13th Street Gainesville, FL 32609-3498 (904) 392-1711; outside Florida (800) 327-4218

Independent Study Program

Fernbank Science Center provides high school students with the opportunity to investigate specific areas of science. Students work closely with expert instructors as they delve into topics that interest them. These course offerings include animal behavior, spider biology, scanning electron microscopy, stream ecology, aeroscience, astronomy, and coastal studies, as well as a host of other choices. Advanced Placement chemistry and physics, and Physical Sciences Study Committee (PSSC) Physics, are also offered at Fernbank. Participants work in well-equipped laboratories and take field trips to study plants and animals in their natural habitats. ***Contact Fernbank for current offerings and registration information.***

Host School:	Fernbank Science Center
Type:	Independent Study Science Enrichment Classes
Location:	Atlanta, GA
Duration:	Three months
Dates:	Courses are offered during the fall, winter, and spring.
Qualifications:	The program is open to interested students from the Dekalb County, Georgia, school system
Housing:	None
Costs:	No charge to students
Credits Given:	Five high school credit hours of science per quarter. College credit for A.P. courses.
Contact:	Independent Study Program
	Fernbank Science Center
	156 Heaton Park Drive, NE
	Atlanta, GA 30307
	(404) 378-4311

Student Profile

Joel Rosner
Miami Beach, Fla.
Self-initiated Law Internship

Joel served as an intern at the Dade County State Attorney's Office during the summer before his senior year. His account is representative of the internship experience during both the summer and school year.

This summer, I interned in a program which I created myself. I was looking for a program that would let me work in a law office. Seeing that there was no such program in existence, I approached the guidance counselor in my school and told her I was interested in working in a law program somewhere. She got me an interview with the state prosecutor's office, and I went to work at the Dade County State Attorney's Office.

I am interested in criminal law, so I decided to work there to see what really goes into being a prosecutor. I also wanted to work somewhere where I was more than a secretary, someplace where I might actually do things that a lawyer might. At the SAO's office, I was able to do that. I did do some filing, but I also called witnesses, sat in on depositions, and wrote case summaries. I also attended court every day, seeing how courts really work. The only drawback to the program was that I was the only person there who was still in high school. Most interns there were law students.

At the end of my internship, I had learned a number of things. For example, I learned about all the work that goes into prosecuting a simple case of cocaine possession and about why the court system is a revolving door. The work I did for the lawyer I interned for showed me the unglamorous side of law: the hours of preparing for any case, the mounds of files to process, the tedium of preparing case after case. Before my internship at the SAO's office, all I ever saw of law and lawyers was on TV shows and in the occasional article, all of which dramatized the exciting parts, the courtroom battles, and the legal parrying. But I had never seen the researching that the lawyers did to find the information they used and the piles of documents they have to read. Going to the SAO's office made me realize that being a lawyer is a great job, but a lot of work. Before I came to the prosecutor's office, I knew I wanted to be a lawyer, but my reasons were based on the version we see in the media. Afterwards, I still wanted to be a lawyer, but now my desire was based on real reasons, on seeing what really goes into law.

Investigations Series

The Investigations Series conferences allow academically gifted students an opportunity to explore a variety of fields of study, college majors, and careers. Students choose workshops in a selection of areas, including investigations in business, family and consumer sciences, design, arts and sciences, and engineering. For example, students interested in business might attend workshops that focus on finance, apparel merchandising, small-business management and entrepreneurship, and organizational behavior. Students interested in design might find themselves in workshops featuring ceramics, calligraphy, computer graphics, and gender issues. Time is set aside during the conference for students to talk with college representatives about their field of interest. Parents and educators may attend special sessions concerning issues for gifted students and college planning. Registrations are accepted on a first-come, first-served basis, so early registration is advised. ***Registration deadline for fall conference: Early October.***

Host School:	Iowa State University
Type:	Conferences for Gifted and Talented Students, their parents, and educators
Location:	Ames, IA
Duration:	One day
Dates:	Two conferences are held each year, one in the fall and one in the spring.
Qualifications:	Students currently in grades 7 through 10. The program is directed toward gifted and talented students, their parents, and teachers. Students may register individually or as a group.
Housing:	None
Costs:	$10 for Iowa Talent Search participants, $15 for non-Iowa Talent Search participants. School groups can attend for $5 per person, with a maximum charge of $50 per group. Parents and educators attend at no charge.
Credits Given:	None
Contact:	Investigations Series
	Iowa State University
	Office of Precollegiate Programs for Talented and Gifted
	W 172 Lagomarcino Hall
	Ames, IA 50011-3810

King-Chavez-Parks Rising Stars (KCP)

The King-Chavez-Parks (KCP) program is designed to increase the number of minority students who pursue postsecondary education. Students attending KCP programs are exposed to a variety of educational and career opportunities, receive academic enrichment instruction, and are encouraged to seek out educational options. Students enter the program through Rising Stars, a series of school year workshops held twice a month on the Michigan State campus. During these workshops, students participate in seminars that consider teen issues such as peer pressure, self-esteem, and stress management. In addition, these seminars cover employability skills, job forecasting, high school and college course selection, college selection and application, and the financial aid process. Students who attend at least six workshops during the school year become eligible for the one-week summer residency program. During this component, students live on campus and get a taste of college life. The students choose two classes each day (one academic, one "fun") from a number offered including such topics as science, communications, leadership, military science, karate, and swimming. A full program of recreational and extracurricular activities, as well as personal growth seminars and college survival workshops, complete this exciting week. ***Contact the program coordinator for information on how to become a "rising star."***

Host School:	Michigan State University
Type:	Academic Year Enrichment and Summer Residency Program
Location:	East Lansing, MI
Duration:	At least six sessions during the school year and a one-week summer residency program.
Dates:	Workshops are held twice a month during the school year. The summer program takes place in July.
Qualifications:	Students currently in grades 6 through 11. The program is designed for minority students (Black, Hispanic, and Native American) interested in opportunities for postsecondary education and careers. Participants come from a 90-mile radius around East Lansing.
Housing:	Participants are housed in dormitories during the summer residency program and are provided with meals. The academic year component is a commuter program.
Costs:	No cost to participants.
Credits Given:	None
Contact:	KCP Rising Stars Michigan State University S-22 Wonders Hall East Lansing, MI 48824-1207 (517) 355-0177

Minnesota Artist Mentor Program

The Artist Mentor Program seeks to enhance student artistic creativity and skill. Students with little or no formal training in the arts and students with extensive artistic backgrounds are encouraged to apply for stipends, allowing them to study with a working professional artist. The study may be in any artistic discipline, including dance, the literary arts, media arts, music, theater, or visual arts. In addition to providing training for students, this program assists practicing area artists financially by employing them as mentors. The awards are made on the basis of the student's commitment to artistic development, motivation, and creative/imaginative thinking ability. *Students may apply through program coordinators in regional high schools or contact the program office for more information.*

Host School:	Minnesota Center for Arts Education
Type:	Training in the Visual and Performing Arts
Location:	Minnesota
Duration:	Variable
Dates:	Throughout the school year and summer
Qualifications:	Students currently in grades 9 through 11. Open to all Minnesota public and private (nonparochial) school students interested in the arts.
Housing:	None
Costs:	Students are awarded stipends to pay for the cost of studying with a professional artist in the discipline of their choice.
Credits Given:	None
Contact:	Minnesota Artist Mentor Program
	Minnesota Center for Arts Education
	6125 Olson Memorial Highway
	Golden Valley, MN 55422
	(800) 657-3515 or (612) 591-4736

National Association of Precollege Directors (NAPD) Programs

The National Association of Precollege Directors (NAPD) is a consortium of 28 precollege program directors who operate minority science and engineering programs in 30 states. All of the programs seek to promote academic achievement and provide enrichment activities to prepare for college study. Although the programs differ, they share common elements including academic enrichment through science clubs, Saturday tutorials, college-based summer programs, and joint high school and college offerings. The individual programs also provide student internships at university and industrial research laboratories, academic advisement and college counseling, career awareness (including field trips and use of professionals as mentors), and science and college fairs. *Contact the chairperson of NAPD to learn about programs operating in your region.*

Host School: Universities and schools across the United States

Type: Academic Enrichment and Career Awareness Programs

Location: Throughout the United States

Duration: Programs offered are of various lengths.

Dates: School year and summer

Qualifications: Programs are open to students in upper elementary grades through grade 12. The programs are directed toward minority students, including African Americans, Hispanics, and Native Americans interested in science and engineering.

Housing: Housing and meals are provided for summer residential programs. School-year programs are held in local communities and are nonresidential.

Costs: No program cost to participants. Many of the programs provide students with a small stipend for their participation.

Credits Given: Some of the summer programs carry college credit.

Contact: Gil Lopez

National Association of Precollege Directors (NAPD) Programs

c/o CMSP

51 Astor Place

New York, NY 10003

(212) 228-0950

New York Academy of Sciences Educational Programs

The Academy presents programs designed to enhance both students' and teachers' understanding of science. Sponsored programs include the New York City School Science and Technology Expo at which students in grades 7 through 12 present science projects and compete for awards, scholarships, and cash prizes. The Science Research Training Program (SRTP) places middle school and high school students as interns with research scientists at a variety of distinguished institutions. The Junior Academy of Science is open to any student in grades 8 through 12 who wants to learn more about science and its applications. Support services for teachers include science seminars for middle and high school teachers and a program bringing scientists from a variety of fields directly into elementary and secondary school classrooms. The Academy also sponsors the Art of Science Competition for students in grades 10 through 12 and participates in the National Science Bowl. ***Contact the Academy for programs, dates, and application information.***

Host School:	The New York Academy of Science
Type:	School Year Science Enrichment Programs
Location:	New York, NY
Duration:	Programs offered are of various lengths
Dates:	Programs are offered throughout the academic year and during the summer months.
Qualifications:	Students in elementary grades through high school. Some programs are limited to students from the metropolitan New York area, while others are open to students across the state or nation. Some programs are directed to teachers.
Housing:	None
Costs:	Most programs are provided at no cost to the student. Some provide a cash stipend.
Credits Given:	Depends upon program chosen
Contact:	New York Academy of Sciences Educational Programs
	The New York Academy of Science
	2 East 63rd Street
	New York, NY 10021
	(212) 838-0230

Nobel Conference

For over thirty years, Gustavus Adolphus College has been the site of officially authorized lecture programs endorsed by the Nobel Foundation. Students have an opportunity to attend a series of lectures by noted scientists, ethicists, and Nobel laureates focusing on a high-level scientific topic. Participants are encouraged to interact with, and ask questions of, the speakers. Recent conferences have been entitled "Nature Out of Balance: The New Ecology" and "Unlocking the Brain: Progress in Neuroscience." The conferences feature interdisciplinary research efforts, introducing a broad range of questions which challenge those working in the field. Speakers at "Unlocking the Brain" included David Hubel, a Nobel laureate in Medicine, noted professors of neurology from the University of Lund, Sweden, Columbia University, the University of Iowa, and Albert Einstein College of Medicine. ***Registration is limited to 3,000 persons per session; early registration is advised.***

Host School:	Gustavus Adolphus College
Type:	Science Enrichment Conference
Location:	Saint Peter, MN
Duration:	Two days
Dates:	Early October
Qualifications:	Students in grades 11 and 12. The program is open to upper level high school students, college and university delegations, and other interested individuals.
Housing:	None
Costs:	$25 for high school, college, and university delegations. Individuals may attend for $10 per person.
Credits Given:	None
Contact:	Nobel Conference
	Gustavus Adolphus College
	800 West College Avenue
	Saint Peter, MN 56082-1498
	(507) 933-7550

①ptions

Chicago State University's Options program provides students of all ages with an array of educational enrichment. Students interested in academics might choose a mathematics or reading improvement class, an ACT review, or an algebra preparatory program. Arts and crafts offerings include such selections as calligraphy, watercolor painting, modeling, designer jewelry, and sewing. Students might choose business and vocational courses from a list that includes word processing, Lotus 1-2-3, shorthand, keyboarding, money management, and office practices. The fine and performing arts are represented through dance (jazz and ballet) and music (piano and voice), writing classes, Spanish language classes, as well as a full range of sports and recreational instruction are also available. ***Contact program office for registration deadlines.***

Host School:	Chicago State University
Type:	Academic Year Enrichment Classes
Location:	Chicago, IL
Duration:	Six weeks
Dates:	Fall and winter terms
Qualifications:	These courses are open to students from elementary age through high school.
Housing:	None. These are commuter classes.
Costs:	$37 to $68 depending upon course chosen.
Credits Given:	None
Contact:	Options
	Chicago State University
	Continuing Education and Nontraditional Programs
	9501 S. King Drive
	Chicago, IL 60628
	(312) 995-2545

Project ICONS! International Communication and Negotiation Simulations

The International Communication and Negotiation Simulations (ICONS) Project is a worldwide, multi-institutional, computer-assisted simulation that thrusts students into the world of high-powered international affairs. The participants assume the role of foreign policy makers, and negotiate through teleconferencing, with different cultures and languages represented. Students consider such global issues as human rights violations, arms control, the balance of trade, nuclear proliferation, the global environment, and international debt. Schools with strong foreign language programs may choose to conduct negotiations in Spanish, French, or German. The simulation itself typically lasts four weeks. United States and foreign teams are linked to the University of Maryland computers, which handle the 2,000 to 3,000 messages exchanged during a simulation. Real-time conferencing allows simultaneous "conversational" negotiation among teams. Only the most basic equipment is needed to participate: a personal computer, printer, modem, and phone line. No prior computer experience is necessary. Several simulations are generally offered each semester, beginning at different times. ***Contact program for participation information.***

Host School: University of Maryland

Type: Interdisciplinary International Relations Program

Location: Program takes place at the student's home school

Duration: One semester (the simulation itself lasts four weeks)

Dates: School year

Qualifications: The program is designed for secondary school students interested in a challenging, international academic experience.

Housing: None. The simulation is conducted via computer network.

Costs: $550 per school and $150 per extra team at the same school. The fee includes mainframe computer costs, a scenario, materials, and technical support.

Credits Given: None

Contact: Professor Jonathan Wilkenfeld
Project ICONS! Department of Government and Politics
College Park, MD 20742
(301) 405-4172; FAX (301) 314-9690

Russia and West Virginia Exchange Program

The Russia & West Virginia Foundation has an established exchange program which seeks to foster increased cultural understanding through the interaction of people, their history, and their traditions. In this cultural exchange program, 20 Russian students and several teachers attend the West Virginia Governor's Schools during the early part of the summer. At the conclusion of the Governor's Schools programs, the Russian students, along with their counterparts from West Virginia, spend time together at a "launching" facility in West Virginia. Following this time, the 15 American students and five teachers travel to St. Petersburg for a one-week cultural and touring program. The students then move on to Kaliningrad, the space center of Russia, where the West Virginia students attend classes and participate in a long weekend cultural exchange through a homestay program with host families. The students also take part in an international math and science Olympiad held at this time in Kaliningrad. The students return with a greater appreciation of cultural differences and similarities. **_Application deadline: March 20._**

Host School:	The Russia & West Virginia Partnership for Exchange, Inc.
Type:	Foreign Exchange Program
Location:	St. Petersburg and Kaliningrad, Russia
Duration:	Three weeks
Dates:	September–October
Qualifications:	Entering grades 11 and 12. Open to outstanding West Virginia students interested in a cultural exchange program. Students qualify through excellent grades and high standardized test scores.
Housing:	Participants stay in a hotel in St. Petersburg and are housed in the dormitories at a study center in Kaliningrad. Meals are provided.
Costs:	No cost to participants.
Credits Given:	None
Contact:	Dr. Virginia Simmons
	Russia and West Virginia Exchange Program
	The Russia and West Virginia Partnership for Exchange, Inc.
	West Virginia Governor's Schools
	Building 6, Room 362, Capitol Complex
	Charleston, WV 25305-0330
	(304) 558-0160; FAX (304) 558-0048

Sargent Camp Internship in Environmental Education

This is a practical training program in the many facets of outdoor environmental education. The internship begins with a two-week training program that includes ropes course techniques, a study of land and water environments, outdoor skills, orienteering, sensory awareness, and night activities. During the program, each intern, paired with a group leader, works with a group of about 10 schoolchildren, in age groups ranging from grade 4 through high school. The groups and programs vary from week to week depending upon theme and grade level. On weekends, interns may participate in workshops held at Sargent Camp in activities such as canoeing, rock climbing, and cross-country skiing. **Contact program office for application information.**

Host School:	Boston University's Sargent Camp
Type:	Internship
Location:	Peterborough, NH
Duration:	One semester
Dates:	Fall semester: Late August to early December.
	Spring semester: Early January through April.
Qualifications:	Interns must be at least 18 years old, committed to the environmental education of children, enjoy being outdoors, willing to work long hours, and have a sense of humor, enthusiasm, and a flexible personality.
Housing:	Interns are provided with onsite housing and meals.
Costs:	None. Interns receive a stipend of $200 per month plus room and board. Weekend work is occasionally available at the rate of $55 per day.
Credits Given:	Credits may be available from the student's school or college.
Contact:	Sargent Camp Internship in Environmental Education
	Boston University's Sargent Camp
	RD #3 Windy Row
	Peterborough, NH 03458
	(603) 525-3311

The Saturday Academy

The Saturday Academy emphasizes building student confidence while increasing competence. Students are provided with role models in science, and parents are enlisted to provide support. University faculty work with young minority students in a college setting providing science enrichment activities. Students gain first-hand experience through laboratory experimentation in the fields of chemistry, physics, and biology. Students may have a chance to work with lasers, to dissect pig embryos, to study pendulum motion, or to compare metric units. Mathematics concepts are taught to improve computational and reasoning skills. In a computer science class, students learn to program in LOGO and BASIC. Special communication skills classes increase the students' communication ability through vocabulary workshops, interview practice, debates, and poetry writing. **Contact program for participation information.**

Host School:	AM-BC/Bennett College
Type:	School Year Science and Communication Skills Enrichment Classes
Location:	Greensboro, NC
Duration:	Twelve Saturday morning sessions are held each semester. The Academy runs from 9 A.M. to 12:10 P.M.
Dates:	Fall and spring semesters
Qualifications:	Students currently in grades 4 through 8. Open to minority students recommended by their school counselor or teacher for participation. Selection is on a first-come, first-served basis.
Housing:	None
Costs:	Participant fees are kept at a minimum. Scholarships for needy students are available.
Credits Given:	None
Contact:	Dr. Nellouise Watkins
	The Saturday Academy
	AM-BC/Bennett College
	900 East Washington Street
	Greensboro, NC 27401-3239
	(919) 370-8684

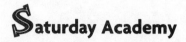

Saturday Academy

Saturday Academy is for students who like to learn in a hands-on, direct way. Informal, project-oriented classes are offered in computing, engineering, physical and biological sciences, communications, business, the humanities, and the arts. Most classes are held on-site where the instructor works or teaches, giving students access to equipment and laboratories used by professionals in their chosen field. Through association with their instructors, students have a chance to "test out" careers and learn firsthand what the profession is all about through their interaction with instructors. Recent offerings have included such courses as an aviation class at Portland International Airport, animation and screenwriting workshops at the Northwest Film Center, architecture at Portland State University, computer-aided design at Hewlett-Packard, courtroom law at Portland State and Multnomah County Courthouse, and computer art and design at Tektronix. Students who take part in the Saturday Academy have learning experiences impossible to duplicate in their home schools. ***Contact program coordinator for registration dates.***

Host School:	Oregon Graduate Institute of Science and Technology
Type:	Academic Year Enrichment Classes
Location:	Programs are presented at local institutions and industrial sites. Most are held at the instructor's workplace, allowing use of professional equipment.
Duration:	One to eight sessions are held; individual sessions might last from one hour to an entire day.
Dates:	Classes are presented on Saturdays, Sundays, and on selected weekday evenings throughout the school year.
Qualifications:	The program is open to all interested students from grades 4 through 12. Classes are grouped by grade level, and a few have prerequisites.
Housing:	None. This is a commuter program for local students.
Costs:	$35 to $150 per course; most course fees are under $100. Tuition assistance is available upon request. No student is turned away because of an inability to pay tuition.
Credits Given:	None
Contact:	Saturday Academy
	Oregon Graduate Institute of Science and Technology
	P.O. Box 91000
	Portland, OR 97291-1000
	(503) 690-1241; FAX (503) 690-1470

Saturday Enrichment Program for Gifted Learners

A wide selection of enrichment classes for gifted learners is given each semester at William and Mary. The program is designed to allow students to explore in greater depth specialized areas of mathematics, the sciences, and the humanities. Classes are limited to no more than 15 students, permitting greater interaction between the instructor, students, and peers. Courses are offered to students in specified grade levels. Offerings for middle school students include German, French, mathematical mind mapping, problem-based science, nuclear energy, archaeology, violence and negotiations, and architecture. *Contact the program coordinator for additional course information and registration deadlines.*

Host School: The College of William and Mary

Type: School Year Enrichment Classes

Location: Williamsburg, VA

Duration: Six weeks

Dates: Fall and spring semesters

Qualifications: Gifted students from preschool (age 4) through grade 8. Participants must have scored at the 95th percentile, or above, on a nationally normed aptitude or achievement test.

Housing: None

Costs: $165 per course. Partial need-based scholarships are available.

Credits Given: None

Contact: Saturday Enrichment Program for Gifted Learners
The College of William & Mary
Center for Gifted Education
P.O. Box 8795, 232 Jamestown Road
Williamsburg, VA 23187-8795
(804) 221-2362; FAX (804) 221-2184

$\mathcal{S}$aturday Scholars Program

Students in Saturday Scholars can explore topics in science and mathematics in greater depth than that which is available at their home schools. Instructional units focus on areas that include the physics of motion, the art of architecture, computer skills, chemical mysteries, and aerospace technology. Each instructional unit provides project-oriented laboratory experiences, with students improving their problem-solving ability and learning skills while confronting real-world problem situations. Participants are encouraged to depend upon each other for peer support as a way of increasing the success of students in secondary mathematics and science coursework. Saturday Scholars are challenged with scientific and mathematical projects that stretch their imagination and creativity, and increase their knowledge base. ***Contact program coordinator for application information.***

Host School:	Rensselaer Polytechnic Institute
Type:	Academic Year Enrichment Classes
Location:	Troy, NY
Duration:	Each session takes place over six Saturday mornings.
Dates:	Sessions are held from October through June
Qualifications:	Students in grades 7 through 12. The program is designed for minority, disadvantaged, and/or gifted and talented students. Separate sessions are held for different levels of students.
Housing:	None. This is a commuter program.
Costs:	None
Credits Given:	None
Contact:	Saturday Scholars Program
	Rensselaer Polytechnic Institute
	Troy Building
	Troy, NY 12180-3590
	(518) 276-6272

Saturday Studios

Saturday Studios offer students of all ages a chance to explore the visual arts. The Studios focus on the formulation of ideas, the handling of materials, and defining and achieving one's goals and objectives. The emphasis in each class is concerned with observation and imagination. Students work with a variety of materials and techniques, including painting, sculpture, and drawing; each studio course is designed around a relevant theme. Instructors take each student's art experience into account when determining the content of the class. Grouped by grade level, courses are available in drawing and painting, printmaking, sculpture, figure drawing, and cartooning. A special course is directed to high school seniors who plan to attend art school. Parents' groups, Saturday morning sessions designed around an exciting speakers program, and museum/gallery visits occur concurrently with Studios. There is no charge for the parents' groups. ***Contact program coordinator for application information.***

Host School:	Massachusetts College of Art
Type:	Art Studio Courses
Location:	Boston, MA
Duration:	Eight Saturday mornings, meeting for two and one-half hours per week.
Dates:	Courses are offered each semester during the academic year.
Qualifications:	These classes are open to all interested students regardless of their level of experience in art.
Housing:	None. This is a commuter program.
Costs:	$65 per course. A limited number of need-based scholarships are available.
Credits Given:	None
Contact:	Saturday Studios
	Massachusetts College of Art
	Art Education Department
	621 Huntington Avenue
	Boston, MA 02115
	(617) 232-1555 ext. 713

Science-By-Mail

In an innovative, international science outreach program, volunteer scientists are teamed with small groups of schoolchildren as the young students attempt to creatively solve a series of scientific challenges. Science-By-Mail sends challenging packets to teams of four students three times during the school year. The packets contain background information about that mailing's subject (photography, cartography, and simple machines were subjects of recent mailings), activities, puzzles, and a central problem. The student groups work on the included activities as they attempt to solve the mailing's "big challenge." If they need expert advice, they can correspond with their scientist—pen pal. Teachers act as coaches; parents can also serve in this role if the program is used as an extracurricular activity. Solutions to problems are sent to "their" scientist; solutions may be presented in writing, on videotape, or in any other form desired by students. The volunteer scientists have a chance to share their enthusiasm with young minds, while students, teachers, and parents gain a new perspective on science. ***Application deadline: November 1.***

Host School: Boston Museum of Science

Type: School Year Science Enrichment Program

Location: The student's home or school

Duration: Academic year

Dates: The program provides three mailings during the school year. Students may spend as much or as little time as desired on each challenge.

Qualifications: Students currently in grades 4 through 9.

Housing: None

Costs: $44 for all materials needed for a team of four students.

Credits Given: None

Contact: Science-By-Mail
Boston Museum of Science
Science Park
Boston, MA 02114-1099
(800) 729-3300

Southeastern Consortium for Minorities in Engineering (SECME) Programs

The largest minority network in the country, the Southeastern Consortium for Minorities in Engineering (SECME) links 30 universities and 65 corporations with 339 schools and almost 16,000 students in nine southeastern states. SECME programs are designed to provide minority students with better academic preparation and a broader field of career options. To this aim, SECME involves teachers, communities, school systems, universities, and industry in the development of local school enrichment programs suited to specific populations. Programs include curriculum enhancement, support programs for academic success (tutoring, parent assistance, self-esteem workshops), career awareness activities, and college admissions and financial aid assistance. ***Contact program director for a full description of programs available.***

Host School:	Georgia Institute of Technology
Type:	School Year Enrichment Programs
Location:	Southeastern United States
Duration:	Programs of varying durations are offered.
Dates:	School year
Qualifications:	The program is directed to students in grades 4 through 12. Participation is open to all students at participating schools, but minority students are especially targeted for SECME programs. Programs are available at selected school districts in Alabama, Florida, Georgia, Kentucky, North Carolina, South Carolina, Tennessee, and Virginia.
Housing:	These are nonresidential programs held at participating schools and universities for local students.
Costs:	No cost to participating students.
Credits Given:	None
Contact:	R. Guy Vickers
	Southeastern Consortium for Minorities in Engineering (SECME) Programs
	Georgia Institute of Technology
	Executive Director SECME
	Atlanta, GA 30332-0270
	(404) 894-3314

"Taking the Road Less Traveled" Career Conference

Each spring, Iowa State's Program for Women in Science and Engineering offers two daylong conferences designed to inform young women, their parents, and teachers about the career opportunities for women in the nontraditional fields of science, engineering, and technology. Participants choose a number of small-group career sessions presented by women professionals, and learn about the day-to-day responsibilities of that profession, educational requirements and planning, and financial returns. Speakers also address the myths and stereotypes associated with women in technical fields, and the significant factors in career preparation. Special resource sessions are directed to parents and educators that offer strategies to encourage and sustain girls' interest in the sciences. Hands-on activity sessions and lab tours complete the day. *Application deadline: early spring, at least one month prior to conference date.*

Host School:	Iowa State University
Type:	Career Education Program
Location:	Ames, IA
Duration:	One day
Dates:	Two sessions are held each spring during March and April. The March session is for grades 6 through 9; the April conference is for grades 9 through 12.
Qualifications:	The program is open to young women currently in grades 6 through 12, as well as their parents and educators.
Housing:	None
Costs:	$12.50 includes the cost of conference and lunch.
Credits Given:	None
Contact:	"Taking the Road Less Traveled" Career Conference
	Iowa State University
	Program for Women in Science and Engineering (PWSE)
	210 Lab of Mechanics
	Ames, IA 50011-2130
	(515) 294-9964

Young Writer's Workshop

The Department of English at Michigan State offers students interested in writing the opportunity to improve their writing skills under the guidance of college students in Michigan State University's teacher preparation programs. During the workshop, each student writes a piece to publish, which is edited by the college students and put into a group anthology. A winter Manuscript Day draws young readers and writers from across the state to share their written work and discuss reading. The Manuscript Day includes a keynote speaker by a young adult author, editorial workshops, and sessions reviewing new book titles for young readers. A paperback book sale and special workshops for parents on how to help their children become better readers and writers are also held. ***Contact the program coordinator for more information.***

Host School:	Michigan State University
Type:	Writing Workshops
Location:	East Lansing, MI
Duration:	One day
Dates:	School year
Qualifications:	Students in grades 4 through 9. The program is open to students interested in writing.
Housing:	None. This is a commuter program.
Costs:	$10
Credits Given:	None
Contact:	Young Writer's Workshop
	Michigan State University
	Department of English
	East Lansing, MI 48824
	(517) 355-7560

Index to Programs by State and Region

Index to Programs by Subject

Index to Special Programs

Index to Programs for Special Populations